JUDSON CORNWALL

LET US BE
Holy

LOGOS INTERNATIONAL
Plainfield, New Jersey

LET US BE HOLY

Copyright © 1978 by Logos International

All rights reserved

Printed in the United States of America

Library of Congress Catalog Card Number: 78-70993

International Standard Book Number: 0-88270-278-5

Logos International, Plainfield, New Jersey 07060

Table of Contents

To my grandchildren:
Marion, Monica, Darlene, Esther, David, Adrian
Judson, and Christian Edward.

I imparted some genetic likeness to each of them, but no divine holiness. This they must obtain from God on their own.

Preface

It is declared by secular historians that the great evangelical movement, in which the doctrine of entire sanctification was so prominent, saved England from a violent political revolution like that which convulsed France the last years of the eighteenth century. The truth of sanctification certainly changed the lives of John and Charles Wesley and George Whitefield, and they in turn changed the lives and times of countless thousands.

In contrast to this, what impact has the present charismatic move had upon the nations it has infiltrated? Perhaps it is too early to measure, but to some of us there seems to be at least one necessary ingredient missing: holiness. It may not be popular, but it is powerful. Without it we shall see neither God nor a revelation of his glory.

I am fully aware that the very use of the terms holiness and sanctification cause some to draw their theological swords and prepare for combat, while others prefer to take to the woods. But if we are as close to the end of time as many think we are, we had better come to grips with the scriptural teaching on this theme, for we claim to be headed toward a holy heaven to spend eternity in the presence of a holy God. Do we realize that "our God is a consuming fire"? Isaiah, who had seen God in his heaven, asked the question, "Who among us shall dwell with the devouring fire? who among us shall dwell with everlasting burnings?" (Isa. 33:14). We need to become aware that holiness is not an attitude of God; it is an attribute of God, an energy so forceful that He cannot help repulsing anything that is inconsistent with the divine nature.

This book is not the history of holiness movements, nor is it an attempt to propound or refute holiness teachings. It is a chronicling of some of my discoveries as I have searched to know and attain the holiness of God.

I do not write from the position of one who has arrived, but as a pilgrim who is still on the journey. Nor have I sought to burden the reader with the processes God put me through in order to teach me some of these things, for that would be a book in its own right. I merely share some of the conclusions I have come to, some of the observations I have made, some of the insights God has given, and some of the writings of other men that have made an impact upon me for holiness.

I hope that the truths shared here will cause some to step out of their fears of the unknown and start walking in the paths of holiness.

Acknowledgments

This book was not my idea. I want to thank Viola Malachuk of Logos International for urging me to write it, and for her encouragement.

I also want to express my deep appreciation to Craig Lawson for the long hours he spent in editing this work and for his insistence that the original manuscript be revamped.

My thanks to my secretary, Cheryl Tipon, who edited the work with a skilled eye for proper grammar, spelling, and punctuation. All of this was heaped upon her regular responsibilities as executive secretary to a church with several ministers on staff.

Likewise, thanks go to Laurel Watson of Eugene, Oregon, for typing and proofing the manuscript.

Special thanks are deserved by and hereby given to my wife, Eleanor, who helped bear the burden of this book with me. She has confided in others that she dreads seeing me begin a book, for she loses me until it is complete. Now she has me back again, for a while.

Section I

THE CHARACTER OF HOLINESS

For I am holy.

1 Peter 1:16

CHAPTER ONE

"Holiness, Anyone?"

The tones of the six-manual Estey pipe organ were still pulsating through my body as the accomplished organist finished the last line of the majestic hymn, "Holy, Holy, Holy." The congregation had sung all four verses of this great tribute to the essential holiness of God with such feeling that the pastor had directed the organist to play an additional verse as the people reverently meditated upon the words. "Blessed trinity" was still stirring in my mind when the choir director stepped onto his small raised platform to signal the robed choir to stand at attention. Once the organist had changed his stops and had indicated his readiness, the director signaled the choir to begin singing, "Take time to be holy, speak oft with thy Lord. . . ."[1] The arrangement was beautiful, and the performance was flawless, but I wondered at the sincerity of the singers. In this generation, who wants to be holy?

It would be easy to believe, in the light of stories of ministerial immorality with women of the congregation, that ministers and pastors do not yearn for holiness. The ordination of homosexuals and lesbians to the priesthood

3

does not seem to reflect a cry for holiness; neither do the questionable business practices and the heavy emphasis upon the possession of *things* so commonplace in the lives of many of God's leaders. The Elmer Gantrys of Hollywood fame are still with us in real life, performing their charlatanry under the guise of spiritual ministry, and the gullible still hand over their life savings and monthly support to these manipulators.

"Take time to be holy," the second verse continued, "the world rushes on; spend much time in secret with Jesus alone." Is this the price of holiness? Then no wonder no one wants it. Who has time to spend with Jesus? Certainly not the ministers. They are so busy with committees, fund raisings, banquets, visitations, counseling sessions, weddings, and funerals that they barely have time to scratch out a Sunday morning sermon. Over the years of talking and counseling with pastors I have rarely found a man who regularly spent an hour a day in intimate fellowship with his Lord. Most of them explain that they "pray while driving the car." This could explain why there seems to be more preaching on "let us own Cadillacs" than on "let us see Jesus."

Certainly if the paid professional of the congregation cannot find time to be holy, it would seem inconceivable that those who had paid him would take the time to attain a realm of holiness higher than their leader. If it is not needful in the priest, it is not needful in the people. In fact, holiness must be the least sought after commodity in the world.

"By looking to Jesus, like Him thou shalt be," the choir continued to sing. But that is not the emphasis of today's ministry. Who even thinks about being like Jesus? We are concerned with brotherhood, fellowship, community, submission, faith for possessions, and a better sex life.

"Holiness, Anyone?"

Check the titles in a Christian bookstore. They'll reveal that we're willing to look at our fat, failures, impotence, and importance, but who buys a book to direct his attention to Jesus? We have conferences on spiritual gifts, family life, finances, and healing for soul and body, but when was the last time you read an advertisement for a conference on holiness? Doesn't anyone want to be like Jesus? Or does the price seem to be too high, or the goal too inaccessible?

"Thy friends in thy conduct His likeness shall see," the soprano section sang as they concluded verse two. Is that what our friends see in our lives? Really? Haven't we watched a generation of young people reject the church because of the hypocrisy they discerned in the members? They refused our plastic, deceitful pretense. They couldn't handle our songs of holiness when they were so aware of our unholy lives. They could not become enthusiastic over the prayer of the deacon on Sunday when they knew that he had beaten his wife on Saturday, nor did the morning soloist move them godward when they knew she was cheating on her husband during the week. They were seeking the truth, but they did not find it amid the trappings of religion that had not changed the lives of the participants. They were looking for someone who could reveal Jesus in everyday living. When they found such a man they flocked to his home or his church in great numbers. Like the visiting Greeks of Jesus' day, they were crying, "Sir, we would see Jesus" (John 12:21).

The choral arrangement called for the male section to lead off on the fourth verse. "Take time to be holy, be calm in thy soul; each thought and each motive beneath His control," they sang. The timbre of their voices was majestic, but their message was archaic. In a day when

5

LET US BE HOLY

Valium and meprobamate are taken by millions of people daily to help calm their nerves, and when drugs and alcohol are used so commonly by all ages as to almost be accepted behavior, who thinks of calmness as something the individual can produce by an act of his will? We have almost routinely accepted this generation's premise that we are creatures totally controlled by our passion and pride, and that we are victims of sensuality and greed. How, then, would we identify with ". . . each thought and each motive beneath His control"?

In the few churches where holiness is still a part of their preached doctrine, they may well sing, "Each *word* and each *action* beneath His control," for the emphasis of most holiness congregations has been on the exterior, not the interior. They have spoken much of manifestation, but little of motivation. They systematize a dress code but not a desire code. But Jesus always seemed to deal with what was in a man's heart; He was far more concerned with "why" than with "what" in the individual's life. Is our materialistic, scientific society ready to come to grips with morals, motives, thoughts, and desires? Are our churches ready to face the sin question squarely and seek a change of heart? Are our pastors and full-time Christian workers prepared to allow the Holy Spirit to strip away the garments of self-righteousness that have clothed them and stand bare and naked before the presence of a living God? Are we disposed to allow the indwelling Spirit that has so excited us in these past few years to have access to our inner sanctum; to allow him to direct our wills, to correct our wants, and to distinguish between love and lust in our lives? Are we sufficiently motivated by heaven's standards to desire holiness, or are we satiated with earth's standards of selfishness?

In speaking to a group of women at the Keswick

convention in England some years ago, Ruth Paxson began by asking, "Do you want to be holy? Perhaps some of us here are defeated; we want to be victorious. We are enslaved; we want to be delivered. We are spiritually tired; we want rest. We are discouraged; we want peace. We are sorrowful; we want joy. But do we have a sense of the utter uncleanness of our lives so that the deepest cry of our heart is for holiness?

"Let us be honest. We must have come to Keswick for something. We must have come because we have a consciousness of some real need. But what is that we want? Do we want to be holy? This is what God wants for us more than anything else. He wants us to be victorious, to be delivered, to be restful, to be joyous, and He has made provision for every one of these blessings for us in the Lord Jesus Christ. But above everything else in this world, He wants us to be holy."[2]

All of this poured through my mind as the choir finished its special number and filed out through doors on either side of the choir loft. Having performed their ministry for the week, they slipped out of their vestments and quietly found places to sit among the congregation. I wondered, is that the way we treat personal holiness? Do we put holiness on as a garment when we have a service to perform and then lay it aside for something more comfortable when our little task is finished? Do we give beautiful lip service to being holy as the trained director leads us, only to disperse into the mass of humanity so unchanged that our presence is unnoticed by those whose lives we touch? Are we a choir singing songs of holiness, or are we a holy people living holy lives? Does our holiness depend upon the mass effect of others harmonizing with our efforts, and does it require the vibrant accompaniment of a pipe organ? If so, it doesn't bear even a faint resemblance to the holiness of God.

My thoughts turned again to the service as the pastor invited the congregation to stand and join him in reading the first eight verses of the fourth chapter of First Thessalonians. Some segments of this passage seemed to echo and reecho in the beautiful sanctuary: ". . . how ye ought to walk and to please God . . . for this is the will of God, even your sanctification . . . that every one of you should know how to possess his vessel in sanctification and honour. . . ; for God hath not called us unto uncleanness, but unto holiness. He therefore that despiseth, despiseth not man, but God, who hath also given unto us his holy Spirit."

That last verse so captured my mind that I did not even hear the pastor's prayer. "He therefore that despiseth, despiseth not man, but God, who hath also given unto us his holy Spirit." Since the entire context concerns holiness in the life of the believer, this verse seems to be saying that to despise a holy life is to despise God himself. This is true, of course, since holiness is one of the moral attributes of God's essential nature. If we reject, or refuse his moral nature, we certainly have no right to call upon his mighty name or to expect to have access to his almighty power. God is indivisible. What He is cannot be separated from what He does, and vice versa. It is a holy God who is the merciful God. Can we receive his mercy while rejecting his holiness, when each is equally an attribute of his nature? To despise any part of God is to despise all of him.

Would God classify the vast majority of worshipers in our churches today as despisers? Are we who build the churches, sing the hymns, pray the prayers, and preach the sermons actually despisers of holiness, and thereby despisers of God?

No, I can't believe so. For this same verse declares, "But God, . . . hath also given unto us his holy Spirit." If He catalogues us as despisers of God He would never have given us his Holy Spirit. And how He has given that Holy Spirit to this generation! Surely the prophecy given through Joel, and quoted by Peter on the day of Pentecost, is coming to pass in our generation: "And it shall come to pass in the last days, saith God, I will pour out of my Spirit upon all flesh. . ." (Joel 2:28 and Acts 2:17). It is very likely that more people have been filled with the Spirit in this generation than in any other generation during the earth's history. Some have even gone so far as to suggest that more people have been filled with the Spirit in this generation than in all other generations put together. But why is that so if this is the generation that is uninterested in holiness?

Is it possible, I reasoned to myself, that we have misinterpreted unknowing as uninterested? Have I, even during this service, judged men as unholy who are really men yearning for holiness who are merely uninformed as to the nature and availability of true holiness? How could it be possible to be filled with the Holy Spirit without having an inner craving for holiness? Wouldn't the Spirit himself create such a craving?

Even people who make no claim to Christ have expressed strong desires for at least righteous behavior in public officials. The Watergate affair started this and multiple scandals have followed. Man after man has fallen from public favor because his behavior slipped below the standard of acceptable righteousness for elected officials. In a minimal sense this is a call for holiness.

How much more would we expect to find this desire in the church of the Lord Jesus Christ! While there are some who are playing the game of the hypocrite, there are many more who have deep inner yearnings to really be saints, for that is what the New Testament calls Christians. Why have people given so sacrificially of their time, talents, and finances if it is not to satisfy an inner drive for holiness? Why are thousands of books and tapes purchased and devoured if there is not a hunger for something more than the present status quo? Why do Christians by the thousands travel miles to conventions, camp meetings, and conferences if there is not a yearning for something from God that they do not possess?

"But," you may ask, "if there is such an appetite for divine holiness, why is there seemingly such an aversion to it?"

Perhaps it is because many misunderstand the grace of God. A rather common picture is that the God of the Old Testament is hard and holy, and through the law He demands perfection. Since the standard was too high, people failed; so Jesus came to lower the standards, and to let a band of incompetent failures into heaven through "grace." They say that in the New Testament it is now free and easy. We're saved by grace! But neither sin nor man's failures have ever changed the purposes of God. His call to holiness has never abated. Grace did not come to revoke that call, but to implement it.

Others so emphasize that Christ came to "seek and to save that which was lost" (Luke 19:10) that they have forgotten that this redemption is not complete until He is able "to present you holy and unblameable and unreproveable in his sight" (Col. 1:22). They may want Jesus to repair their lives, to patch a hole here or there, and maybe refurbish a room; but Christ did not come to repair, but to replace. He came to trade his life for ours; to bring our lives to the cross so that He can share his life from the resurrection side of the tomb.

Maybe this is why many hesitate to embrace divine holiness. Some would like to keep their lives pretty much the way they are. They want to hang on to a few pet sins and vices (although, of course, they would never call them that), some habits, attitudes, desires, dishonesties, and grudges. They have observed that if they let Christ start He won't stop until He has finished, for He is committed to our perfection in him. They would like divine holiness if it could be added to their lives instead of replacing it.

But I believe the most compelling reason for the unpopularity of holiness is that it is misunderstood. We have dulled the fascinating edge of the holy life by viewing it as one that is void of all of the pleasures of life. It is the old concept that "everything pleasant is either immoral, illegal, or fattening." Some equate holiness with poverty, and others, with asceticism. For years many have enforced such rigid controls over the lives of others in the name of holiness that they were always out of style in their dress, out of touch with the world in their associations, and unable to participate in any form of amusement or recreation that was not wholly "Christian."

Had this withdrawal from what they called "worldliness" produced true holiness then it would have been of value. But often it produced little more than difference and misery.

But holiness is not intended to make life uncomfortable and unnatural. Actually, the opposite is true. Holy living involves life at its fullest. It is a removal of the negatives and a replacing with the positives of life. True holiness brings us into a love, joy, and peace such as this world cannot know aside from Christ.

Jesus, the holiest man who ever walked on this earth, impressed people as one who really lived, and they were constantly asking him the secret. In fact, the criticism of the Pharisees was that He lived too much to fit in with their concept of religiousness. And this Jesus declared that one of the purposes of his coming was that "we might have life, and have it more abundantly" (John 10:10). Look at those early Christians—they were vibrant, full of joy, throbbing with life, and everywhere they went they spread this life with its overflowing joy. This same is true in the lives of truly holy people today. They are not seen as miserable ascetics but as joyful exhibitors of life at its highest level.

My wandering mind was brought back to church when the pastor raised his voice to declare, "Perhaps what this generation needs the most is a vision of true holiness as it is seen in the nature of God. The fulness of holiness will never be seen in any earthly man; we must go to the God-man, Christ Jesus, to behold this. It is in the heavens, not on the earth, that holiness is exemplified in its highest order. The cry of the church must become, 'Lord, shew us the Father, and it sufficeth us' " (John 14:8).

I heard myself saying "amen!", and as I left the church I made a resolution to restudy the Bible with an eye to seeing the holiness of God the Father, God the Son, and God the Holy Spirit. Maybe the church doesn't need condemnation for her unholiness as much as she needs motivation to true holiness. If we've never seen the true product it is no wonder we have often turned to carnal, shoddy substitutes. Since the best defense against counterfeit money is a good acquaintance with real money, perhaps the best defense against counterfeit holiness will be association with true holiness as seen in God.

CHAPTER TWO

Holiness Defined

No matter how impoverished a person may be, gaining a working knowledge about money is elementary compared to learning the value, availability, and nature of true holiness, for although holiness is mentioned repeatedly throughout the Scriptures there is considerable theological diversity in the biblical understanding of holiness. At times it seems that there is almost an unwillingness to even try to understand the holiness of God, or, perhaps, a lack of personal experience with God's holiness that could enable us to understand at least some shades of its meaning.

While I was writing this book I was privileged to share five days with thirty or so key men, all of whom are involved in the present move of God as pastors, lay leaders, conference directors, or traveling ministers. We ate our meals seated at tables for four, and by choosing a different table at each meal I was able to have at least one meal with each of the brothers. At each meal I asked the same question, "How would you define holiness?"

Only once was I given a definition; "Holiness is

otherwiseness," one man offered. The others shared examples of what holiness was not, or merely admitted that they rarely ask themselves that question.

I do not intend this observation to be a censure of these men of God; it merely illustrates how seldom any of us try to define the very essence of God which the Bible calls "holiness."

Some theologians speak of holiness as the pervading moral attribute of God's nature, while others insist that it is not one attribute among the other attributes, but is the innermost reality to which all others are related.

The Interpreter's Dictionary of the Bible says, "Even the sum of all the attributes and activities of the holy is insufficient to exhaust its meaning, for to the one who has experienced its presence there is always a plus, a 'something more,' which resists formulation or definition. Its connotations are as diverse as the cultures which seek to describe its mysterious nature, but common to all is an awareness of an undefined and uncanny energy, a sense . . . of the imponderable and incomprehensible, an inarticulate feeling of inviolable potency outside and beyond, removed and distant, yet at the same time near and 'fascinating,' invading the everyday world of normal experience" (Vol. 2, page 616).

Holiness, then, certainly extends into every area of existence, for in the Bible it appears as related to almost everything in the realm of human experience and conduct.

This is to be expected, of course, since wherever God's presence is felt, men encounter the wonder and mystery of holiness, and it effects changes in them, their relationship to life, and their destinies. Furthermore, when God's holiness sets a man apart unto divine service he and the whole pattern of his life is changed forever. The priesthood is a well-known example.

Sometimes when the Scriptures speak of holiness it is used in a moral sense, and other times it has little ethical connotation. Whatever was devoted to God and his service was declared "holy" whether it be people ("holy prophets"), property ("holy ark"), or places ("holy city"). This did not necessarily signify that they were partakers of God's nature, but that they had been separated unto his use. They were holy because they belonged to the Holy One.

When the context signifies that a moral or ethical sense is intended we gain a far greater insight into the meaning of holiness, for usually the accompanying passage includes words and phrases that help to define, explore, and enlarge our concept of holiness. These give us both color and contrast, and express the positive and negative factors in holiness. Trying to explain holiness without these verbal shades of meaning is akin to trying to describe the beauty of a sunset by using only the words "black and white."

The subject of holiness is hardly introduced in the Bible before we see fire connected with the manifestation of God's person. Moses first met God in the burning bush, and Isaiah's great transformation came after the seraphim, "the fiery ones," antiphonally chanted "Holy, holy, holy," before the throne of God, and his cleansing was with a coal of fire from the altar of God. The New Testament goes so far as to declare, "Our God is a consuming fire" (Heb. 12:29). Nouns that speak of fire are commonly connected with holiness in the Old Testament: "light," "heat," "smoke," "flame," "coals," "furnace," "caldron," "ashes," and "brimstone." Similarly the verbs reflect this same symbolism: "scorch," "blaze," "consume," "burn," "kindle," "glow," "warm," "quench," and so forth. In the Book of Acts the initial outpouring of the Holy Spirit was accompanied with "cloven tongues like as of fire, and it sat upon each of them" (Acts 2:3). So fire is interconnected with the manifestation of God's holiness.

This "fire" description of God's holiness is also coupled with jealousy: ". . . God is a consuming fire, even a jealous God" (Deut. 4:24). It belongs to the nature of God to maintain the uniqueness and integrity of his deity, and this is revealed in the passionate zeal and drive of his holy being described in Scripture as jealousy. The energy and force of his holy jealousy is so great that at times it seems to be almost identical with holiness itself. His very name is "Jealous" (Exod. 34:14), and, as *The Interpreter's Dictionary of the Bible* says, "His unpredictable passionateness, the drive of the divine pathos, is intimately involved with his jealousy, and expresses the vitality and intense urgency of his holy activity. It is in this context that we must read passages which refer to Yahweh's 'hate' " (Vol. 2, page 618).

Such a holy, jealous God demands exclusive worship; He cannot tolerate worship that is in defiance of his essential and innermost nature.

Since worship is basically man's response to God's manifested holiness, such a holy, jealous God demands exclusive worship. Furthermore, He cannot tolerate worship that is in defiance of his essential and innermost nature.

Such idolatry and false worship incurs the wrath of God throughout the Scriptures. Even nations who do not seem to have had a revelation of the holiness of God were severely judged for their unholy worship and their worship of the unholy. God's wrath is closely connected with his holiness.

Partially because of this, and mostly because any

manifestation of God is so beyond our present level of understanding as to be awe-inspiring, the biblical understanding of holiness includes the broad sphere of dread, terror, awe, reverence, and fear. God is viewed as awesome and terrible, and the shades of meaning that the contexts provide speak of majesty, sublimity, augustness, and reverence.

Holiness and fear are interrelated, but it is not the fear that demon worshipers experience, that dread of supernatural punishment or wrath, as much as it is a response to the revelation of the great distance that exists between man and God. Our concepts of God fall far short of reality since there is nothing on earth with which to compare God, so when He reveals an area of his majestic holiness it produces a sense of wonder not too unlike that which blind Bartimaeus must have experienced when he viewed his first sunrise after Jesus gave him his sight.

This very awareness of the division between the human and the divine is, in itself, an explanation of holiness. The holy is unapproachable; man must not come near to it, as Moses learned at the burning bush, and Israel learned at Mount Sinai. While no man may see God and live (Exod. 33:20), the men of Bethshemesh, who lifted the mercy seat to peer into the ark upon its return from Philistine captivity, learned that even looking upon God's holy things can perpetrate a great slaughter. The survivors cried out in terror, "Who is able to stand before this holy Lord God?" (1 Sam. 6:20). God is God and man is man. The very awareness of this is a part of our understanding of holiness. We should not "humanize" God in our concepts nor "deify" ourselves. None who have experienced the holiness of God would try to "play God," for he has seen the holy and knows that the profane can never be elevated sufficiently to become even a weak substitute.

Paralleled to the contrast between "holy" and "profane" is the antithesis between "clean" and "unclean" through the Scriptures. The relation between the two contrasts is so intimate as often to suggest identical meanings but they are not truly synonymous, for purity or cleanness is an aspect of holiness. Whenever God's holiness is made available to man, whether in ritual or reality, cleanness is an integral part. In the tabernacle worship frequently sprinklings and washing were a vital part of the worship of the Lord, and in the moral sense we are taught that "The blood of Jesus Christ his Son cleanseth us from all sin" (1 John 1:7). David petitioned God to, "purge me with hyssop, and I shall be clean: wash me, and I shall be whiter than snow . . . blot out all mine iniquities. Create in me a clean heart, O God" (Ps. 51:7, 9, 10). He knew that holiness and cleanness were inseparable.

Similarly, holiness and majesty interrelate in describing the quality and character of holiness. Of God it is said that He is clothed with majesty (Ps. 93:1); that honor and majesty go before him (Ps. 96:6); that his voice is full of majesty (Ps. 29:4); and that his name is majestic in all the earth (Ps. 8:1 RSV). In the New Testament Peter declares, ". . . but [we] were eyewitnesses of his majesty. For he received from God the Father honour and glory . . ." (2 Pet. 1:16, 17), while Jude ascribes majesty to God in his closing benediction: "To the only wise God our Saviour, be glory and majesty, dominion and power, both now and ever. Amen" (Jude 25).

Because God and holiness are inseparable there is a vast reservoir of words used in the Bible to describe it. Our holy God is "wonderful," his very name is "Wonderful" (Isa. 9:6), and what He does is declared as wonderful. He is also "great" and his acts are seen as "great" acts. He is exalted—"high and lifted up" (Isa. 6:1), and called the "Most High." Similarly, God and holiness are described by such words as, "goodness," "pleasantness," "reverence," "power," "honor," "exaltation," "supremacy," and "loftiness." None adequately describes God's holiness, but each contributes something further to our concept.

But if there is one singular thing about the holiness of God that stands out above all others it is probably that holiness is unsearchable, incomprehensible, and incomparable. The deep things of God cannot be fathomed by man for the limits and mysteries of his ways are beyond our wildest imaginations. The Psalmist declared, "Such knowledge is too wonderful for me; it is high, I cannot attain unto it" (Ps. 139:6). Since his day vast libraries have been assembled, man's knowledge has expanded unbelievably, and intricate computers make knowledge available to men almost instantly. But we still do not understand the holiness of God.

God has always been and will always be incomparable in his holiness. His holiness cannot be fashioned in anything that man can see. He has always been the invisible sovereign. There is none among the gods like him in his holiness (Exod. 15:11), for his uniqueness is the uniqueness of his holiness. Therefore, all comparisons are futile. God is in heaven and man on earth, and man has nothing in his realm with which to compare God. He is distinctively holy.

CHAPTER THREE

Holiness as Seen in the Godhead

God the Father

When Paul quoted the Old Testament in saying, "Eye hath not seen, nor ear heard, neither have entered into the heart of man, the things which God hath prepared for them that love him," he added, "But God hath revealed them unto us by his Spirit" (1 Cor. 2:9, 10). All knowledge of God and his holiness must come through his self-revelation, and this revelation is progressive.

The very first time the word holiness is used in the Bible is in the song of Moses right after the Lord had slain the Egyptian army in the sea, thereby delivering Israel from her enemy. Moses led the Israelites in singing, "Who is like unto thee, O Lord, among the gods? who is like thee, *glorious in holiness*, fearful in praises, doing wonders?" (Exod. 15:11, emphasis added). The Revised Standard Version translates the expression as "majestic in holiness."

Commenting on this, Matthew Henry wrote, "His holiness is his glory," while Adam Clark said, "[God was] infinitely resplendent in this attribute, essential to the perfection of the divine nature."[3] But it is the writing of Dr. Robert Jamieson that expands these concepts. He said, "No attribute in the character of the true God presents a more striking contrast to the low and groveling qualities ascribed to the heathen deities than His purity or righteousness. It is the brightest jewel in the crown of the Divine Majesty, shedding a lustre on all his other perfections, and being that which most of all exalts Him in the estimation of all His intelligent and moral creatures."[4]

So very early in the Holy Scriptures God is declared and described as being holy, entirely separated from anything and everything that is inconsistent with his purity and righteousness.

Through the pages of the Old Testament God unveiled his nature by adding a descriptive word or phrase to his sacred, eternal name. To Abraham He revealed himself as *Jehovah-jireh*, "the Lord will provide" (Gen. 22:14); to Israel He sealed his pledge with the compound name *Adonai-Rapah*, "the Lord that healeth" (Exod. 15:26), and unveiled himself further as, "the Lord is my banner" (Exod. 17:15); "the Lord is peace" (Judg. 6:24); "the Lord our shepherd" (Ps. 23:1); "the Lord our righteousness" (Jer. 23:6), and to Ezekiel, separated from his beloved homeland, came the revelation of *Jehovah-Shammah* "the Lord is present" (Ezek. 48:35).

But it was to the prophet Isaiah that God gave the higher revelation that his very name is "Holy." "For thus saith the high and lofty One that inhabiteth eternity, whose name is Holy . . ." (Isa. 57:15). This is certainly far more than merely declaring that his name was hallowed, or set apart; it is as much a revelation of the divine nature of God as any of the prior revelations of God's name. God is not only the provider, the healer, the banner, the peace, the shepherd, the righteousness, or the present one; He is also the Holy One. It is intrinsic to his nature, not merely descriptive of his attitudes. "I am holy" is as distinctive a part of his nature as "I am the Lord that healeth thee," and as much a part of his provision for mankind as "the Lord is my shepherd." More than twenty times the Bible speaks of God's "holy name."

From the beginning of his ministry to the closing pages of his book, Isaiah perceives and proclaims the holiness of God; a holiness that is not so much a moral quality as it is the expression of the Godhead in the absolute sense. "Holy, holy, holy *is* the Lord of hosts," the seraphim chanted one to another (Isa. 6:3, emphasis added). This is *what* He is, not *how* He functions.

Of course, all attempts to define God meet with frustration, and godly scholars throughout the ages have sought to reduce God's limited revelation of himself to a creed or statement of faith. But in their attempts to broaden our understanding of God they often speak of God as possessing both natural and moral attributes. Usually they list four attributes in each category. Some feel that such a division should not be made and that these qualities of God, which some call attributes, are, in reality, part of His nature and essence. But the purpose of listing the attributes of God is simply to separate the essential nature of God from these qualities called attributes.

Under *natural attributes* are generally listed God's *omniscience* (He is all knowing), God's *omnipotence* (He is all powerful), God's *omnipresence* (He is everywhere present), and God's *eternity* and *immutability* (He is of infinite duration and is unchangeable). It is difficult to form a concept of God without an awareness of these four fundamental characteristics of his nature.

But there are moral attributes that are as fundamental to our understanding of God as these natural attributes.

They are generally listed as the *holiness* of God, the *righteousness* and *justice* of God, the *mercy* and *lovingkindness* of God, and the *love* of God. These moral qualities are as much a part of the intrinsic nature and essence of God as are the natural attributes.

In the book *The Great Doctrines of the Bible* by Rev. William Evans, he says, "If there is any difference in importance in the attributes of God, that of His Holiness seems to occupy the first place. It is, to say the least, the one attribute which God would have His people remember Him by more than any other. In the visions of Himself which God granted men in the Scriptures the thing that stood out most prominent was the divine holiness. This is clearly seen by referring to the visions of Moses, Job, and Isaiah."[5]

Later in the book Rev. Evans says, "The holiness of God is the message of the entire Old Testament. To the prophets, God was the absolutely Holy One; the One with eyes too pure to behold evil; the One swift to punish iniquity. In taking a photograph, the part of the body which we desire most to see is not the hands or feet, but the face. So it is with our vision of God. He desires us to see not His hand and finger, denoting His power and skill, nor even His throne as indicating His majesty. It is His holiness by which He desires to be remembered, as that is the attribute which most glorifies Him. Let us bear this fact in mind as we study this attribute of the divine nature. It is just this vision of God that we need today when the tendency to deny the reality or the awfulness of sin is so prevalent. Our view of the necessity of the atonement will depend very largely upon our view of the holiness of God. Light views of God and His holiness will produce light views of sin and the atonement."[6]

During my Bible school days I was privileged to have

long talks about holiness with a godly missionary to the Mossi tribes of Africa. John Hall had been forced home from Africa for the duration of World War II, so he came to Southern California Bible College as the dean of men and as a teacher. Fortunately for me, he was also my counselor, and he came frequently to my room on the third floor of the annex just to talk about God. He both satisfied my hunger for more of God and then created an even greater hunger for more of the reality of God's presence.

In retrospect I realize that he sensed deep longings in me, and he tried jealously to guard me from anything that would keep me from finding the holy life in God that I yearned after.

Brother Hall used to remind me that God declares that his *name* is holy; therefore, all who desire to be acquainted with him must know him as a holy God. His *nature* is holy, so all who would have fellowship with him must do so in holiness. His very *habitation* is holy, so all who would draw near to him must enter the place of holiness, for in the very same verse where Isaiah declared that God's name is Holy he also declares, ". . . I dwell in the high and *holy place*" (Isa. 57:15, emphasis added). Even at a time when the other deities recognized in the world were conceived of as sunk in sensuality and selfishness, dwelling in places of iniquity and lust, God revealed himself to Isaiah as a holy being whose place of residence was as holy as his person.

No matter what concept is used to symbolize God's dwelling place, all of the Bible emphasizes the holiness of that dwelling. The historic books speak of the *holy of holies* in the tabernacle, and later the temple, as the place of God's residence among men; the poetic books refer to God's *holy hill* (Ps. 99:9), and of his *holy heaven* (Ps. 20:6), while the prophetic books talk more about Jerusalem, the *holy city* (Isa. 4:3) as being the place of God's habitation among men. But the emphasis is always upon the holiness of God's habitation. It is sanctified to God's use, hallowed in man's concepts, and made holy by God's presence. Wherever God is becomes a most holy place, for He dwells "in the holy place."

The New Testament singularly speaks of heaven as being the residence of God and his holy angels, and as being the future home for the church. God has dwelt with man on earth, but man will dwell with God in heaven. But it will require holiness. Even now heaven's residents are called "holy angels" (Mark 8:38; Luke 9:26). God, whose name is holy, not only dwells in a holy place but is surrounded by spiritual beings who are partakers of his holiness.

God's heaven was never made for anything short of absolute holiness. The Book of Revelation indicates that God's heaven is populated with an innumerable company of these glorious beings whose rank determines their nearness to God (or perhaps it is the other way around), but even the lowest ranks of angels is sinless, pure, unsullied, undefiled, innocent, and holy. They are able to worship God in the beauty of holiness because they are beings of holiness. Their actions are holy because their attitudes are holy. They seem to harmonize perfectly with the will of God at all times because they are one in the holiness of God constantly. God is not only "in his holy temple" (Ps. 11:4), but He is surrounded by his holy angels, some of whom, especially the cherubim, exist specifically to guard his holiness.

If God had remained in his holy heaven we would never have known of his holiness or had a chance to share in it. But He didn't remain aloof from men, He came down to men as a man in the person of the Lord Jesus Christ.

God the Son

God "apostled" Jesus to a very special task. "Thy holy child Jesus" (Acts 4:30) was sent forth separated from the glory of heaven and commissioned through divine holiness to remain separate from the sin and ungodliness of this earth. He did not come as a theophanic manifestation (God in angel form), but He became a man without losing the reality of being God.

In discussing divine holiness with Edward Miller, a veteran missionary to South America who has learned so much about personal relationship with God, I asked him what he felt was the chief characteristic of God's holiness.

"His humility," was his answer, "and never was this intrinsic, holy humility of God made more evident than in the coming of the Lord Jesus Christ. It is as natural for God to come down to man's level as it is for a father to lower himself to the level of his small child, but in the coming of Jesus, God more than lowered himself to meet a child; He humbled himself to become that child."

The *Zondervan Pictorial Encyclopedia* says, "[Humility] is a virtue to which other religions accord no honor, and even fail to recognize. Philosophers, except those positively influenced by the Judeo-Christian tradition, likewise ignore or belittle it" (Vol. 3, page 222).

The Scriptures teach that humility is a quality ascribed to God himself. The Psalmist affirms, "Who is like unto the Lord our God, who dwelleth on high, *who humbleth himself* to behold the things that are in heaven, and in the earth" (Ps. 113:5, 6, emphasis added).

In the Megilla (31, a) an ancient Jewish writer says, "Wherever the Scripture bears witness to the Divine mightiness, it brings out side by side with it the Divine humbleness." Humility and holiness not only coexist; they coinhere. While God's holiness completely separated him from all that is evil, impure, sinful, or morally imperfect, his humility has caused him to make himself both known and available to the unholy and the defiled.

One beautiful theme that is found throughout all of the Bible is that God has consistently lowered himself to have fellowship with man, though not in the sense of compromising his holy nature. It is not the king playing the commoner, as in *The Prince and the Pauper*, but it is the king associating with the commoner with such humility in his position that he can make everyone comfortable in his presence. Of Jesus it was said, "The common people heard him gladly" (Mark 12:37).

Paul expressed it, "[Christ], being in the form of God, thought it not robbery [a thing to be coveted, or grasped after] to be equal with God: But made himself of no reputation, and took upon him the form of a servant, and was made in the likeness of men: And being found in fashion as a man, *he humbled himself*, and became obedient unto death, even the death of the cross" (Phil. 2:6-8, emphasis added). God's only begotten Son came down neither to condemn nor to condone, but to change men into the very image of Christ. But to do so He had to become a man.

Jesus Christ was not just a great man who achieved such holiness as to be taken into the presence of God; He was the holy one of God who humbled himself to become a man. His holiness was not achieved through the life He lived here on earth; it was inherently his from the beginning, for He, as is the Father, is the Holy One.

This was explained to Mary before the conception of Christ when the angel said, "The Holy Ghost shall come upon thee, and the power of the Highest shall overshadow thee: therefore also *that holy thing* which shall be born of thee shall be called the Son of God" (Luke 1:35, emphasis added). His holiness was transplanted to earth in the miraculous conception. What He was in eternity was merely reduced to a microscopic embryo which was allowed to grow in Mary's womb until it was birthed as a male child in Bethlehem of Judea. As the child matured into manhood the holiness was manifested at higher and higher levels, but its origin was in the eternal heavens with the Father.

That Jesus was indeed the Holy One of God was demonstrated repeatedly during his lifetime. At his baptism John declared, ". . . This is the Son of God" (John 1:34); during his ministry demons declared him to be, ". . . The Holy One of God" (Luke 4:34), and the early church prayed, ". . . That signs and wonders may be done by the name of thy *holy child Jesus*" (Acts 4:30, emphasis added). At Jesus' death the centurion who supervised the crucifixion declared, "Truly this man was the Son of God" (Mark 15:39), and in Christ's resurrection his holiness was finally confirmed once and for all. David had prophesied, and Peter and Paul quoted it, ". . . Thou shalt not suffer thine Holy One to see corruption" (Ps. 16:10; Acts 2:27; 13:35). Christ's resurrection as the firstfruits of the church proved incontestably that He was the Holy One, the one in whom was inherent holiness.

Sometimes the human and divine natures of Jesus Christ seem to be incompatible and mutually exclusive, and yet this perfect blend of sinless perfection and fragile humanity was necessary in order to fulfill a divine commission, for Christ was not only the Holy One of God, but was the Sent One from God. Christ was sent from God not as a prophet or priest with a message from God, but to demonstrate, display, and reveal the Father. He had more than a ministry to share; He had a divine nature to show. After all, He was and is God; the Father and Son share the same nature. Jesus attested to this repeatedly in the Gospel of John.

How vividly the Gospels display Christ constantly exemplifying God's holiness. In *his attitudes* there was a consistent love; even for the unlovely, and for his persecutors. Christ was moved with compassion for the shepherdless sheep. His attitude toward the sinners was neither condemning nor condoning; it was compassionate. He was never self-seeking or proud. He was easily entreated, but He could not be deterred from doing the will of God. His only recorded anger was righteous indignation at the desecration of the Father's house of prayer. His holiness did not make him undesirable to people, it seemed to attract people to him. Men loved to be around him, women were comfortable in his presence, and children never seemed to be ill at ease with him.

In *his actions*, Christ displayed God's holiness through his disgust with religious hypocrisy and in his hatred of sin. He so perfectly displayed God's divine holiness that He hated the sin and still loved the sinner. He was always just, but when He met with repentance He became the justifier.

Furthermore, He maintained his apartness from sin without needing complete separation from sinners. Much to the chagrin of the Pharisees, Jesus ate with publicans, fellowshiped with sinners, and ministered to the poor, the unlearned, and the underprivileged. He did not maintain his holiness by separating his person from every unholy influence, but by separating his will to the will of a holy God. Once his heart was established to holiness his actions could be effectual to unholy people without defiling the inner purity of the Son of God. Somehow He did not fear that He might "catch" unrighteousness, for through holiness He had developed an immunity to sin. Rather, He became a "carrier" of divine righteousness and He infected people everywhere He went.

This constant exemplification of God's holiness is equally evident in his teaching ministry, for He did not come to expound the law of Moses but to express the principles of God's kingdom. Christ powerfully proclaimed the route into divine holiness. In the Sermon on the Mount Jesus taught about the Christians' responsibilities in their relationship to the world in declaring that they should become the "salt of the earth" and "the light of the world" (Matt. 5:13-16). He showed how important it was to live obediently to the word of God (Matt. 5:17-20), and began a series of teachings that use the contrasting statements, "Ye have heard that it was said by them of old time . . . but I say unto you . . . ," in them revealing that while the law and the prophets may define proper action, God's holiness demands proper attitudes. He defined motivation as more important to God than manifestation, and thereby He removed all of the grounds of self-righteousness which declare that if a man does the right things he is holy. Jesus taught that if a man is holy he will automatically do the right things.

I also saw that in dealing with the need for a proper inner attitude, Jesus taught men how to handle anger (Matt. 5:21, 22); broken relationships (Matt. 5:23-26); sexual purity (Matt. 5:27-32); oaths (Matt. 5:33-37); retaliation (Matt. 5:38-42) and love (Matt. 5:43-48). The principles that He was teaching were on a higher plane than the religious discipline of the scribes, Pharisees, or Sadducees since Christ was teaching moral righteousness rather than ceremonial correctness. Even so, his teaching was very practical, for in chapter six Jesus gave righteous instruction about giving (Matt. 6:1-4); praying (vv. 5-15);

money management (vv. 19-23); serving (v. 24); anxiety (v. 25); adornment (v. 28); source of supply (v. 31); and ended the discourse by giving a proper order of priorities for our lives (v. 33).

In all of his teaching Jesus seemed to emphasize that God was more interested in getting heaven into us than in getting us into heaven. "But seek ye first the kingdom of God, and his righteousness," He said, "and all these things shall be added unto you" (Matt. 6:33). He made righteousness such a desirable goal that it was to become the uppermost thought of our minds, the first priority of our lives, and the motivating force for all of our actions. Holiness was the underlying theme of everything that Jesus taught, no matter what the subject may have been.

Christ's reception among men was varied, for few really understood who Jesus actually was. But in spite of the varied interpretations of his office, calling, or person, all were aware of his "other-worldliness"—the divine holiness—of his life. He stood out as the different one in a crowd. There was a magnetism about him that attracted people of all classes and ages to his presence, and such a gentle display of the moral character of God as to be comforting to the distressed and sorrowing as well as challenging to the excited and exuberant. He was received of men not because He wore an identifying sign declaring him to be the Son of God, but because He displayed such righteousness and holiness in his every word and action.

Actually, about the only people who rejected Jesus as a person were the religious hypocrites. The other people received him gladly. Even sinners, whom we might expect to be the most uncomfortable in his presence, could relate to him because his holiness did not condemn their unholiness; it revealed their sin, but also showed compassion and love.

The life of Christ shows that true holiness is attractive to people, not repulsive. It is only self-righteousness, man's filthy substitute for divine holiness, that repels others. It is like offering plastic fruit to a hungry person, or offering a thirsty man a glass of vinegar.

By his life on earth Christ demonstrated that holiness can survive in an unholy environment; that the power of God's holiness is far greater than the power of sin's unholiness; and that men can be infused with God's Holy Spirit and learn to develop holy lives. So before leaving this earth, Christ promised to send the same Spirit of holiness that had indwelt and motivated him, pledging that this Spirit would reside in his disciples, and all receptive believers, so that they might have access to the same holiness that was manifested in Christ Jesus our Lord.

God the Spirit

It is interesting to me that while the Scriptures do not often refer to God as "the Holy Father," nor to Jesus as "Holy Jesus" or "Holy Christ," they rarely speak of the Spirit of God without calling him "holy." Although He is called "the spirit of glory," "the spirit of grace," "the spirit of judgment," "the spirit of knowledge," and "the spirit of meekness," all of these titles combined occur less than ten times in the Bible; furthermore, He is called "the Spirit of God" less than thirty times. Yet He is titled "the Holy Spirit" nearly a hundred times, for the Holy Spirit is as much a partaker of the divine nature of the Godhead as is the Father. He is holy not because of the name they gave to him, but they gave that name to him because He is inherently holy. The basic characteristic of his moral nature is holiness. He, as much as the Father and the Son, is intrinsically set apart from all evil, is immanently separated from every form of defilement, and is indigenously pure, righteous, and holy. His predisposition is a love for righteousness and a hatred for sin. He has natural holiness, not nurtured holiness; that is to say, his holiness is characteristic of him, not conferred on him. He *is* holy; that's why we call him the *Holy* Spirit.

When the angels of glory gather around the throne to chant, "Holy, holy, holy, Lord God Almighty; which was, and is, and is to come" (Rev. 4:8), they are responding to the Holy Spirit every bit as much as they are worshiping God or his Christ.

He, like Christ, is holy in the sense of being separated unto God's specific service, for his mission and commission is to adapt holiness to mankind thereby effecting radical changes in their natures. Through his mission of regeneration He transforms men from creatures of darkness into creatures of light; by producing the fruit of the Spirit within them He enables men to rise above their human nature and become partakers of the divine nature, and by operating the gifts of the Spirit through them, men are lifted from their impotency into a measure of God's omnipotency—from natural limitations into supernatural limitlessness.

The Spirit of God, then, is holy by name, holy by nature, holy by mission, and holy in his manifestation.

Holiness is equally, but diversely, seen in the Godhead. It is the pervading moral attribute of the Father that was demonstrated on earth in the life of the Son, and is applied in the life of the believer by the Spirit.

Section II

THE COMMITMENT OF HOLINESS

Be ye holy.

1 Peter 1:16

CHAPTER FOUR

Holiness Brought to Earth

Throughout the Old Testament God's display of holiness proved to be more repelling than attractive. When the glory of his holiness filled the temple on the day of its dedication the priests dared not enter "because the glory of the Lord had filled the Lord's house" (2 Chron. 7:2), and when God came down on Sinai prior to the giving of the law, ". . . There were thunders and lightnings, and a thick cloud upon the mount, and the voice of the trumpet exceeding loud; so that all the people that was in the camp trembled" (Exod. 19:16). Gideon expected immediate death after seeing an angel of the Lord (Judg. 6:22, 23), as did other men in the Bible. So traumatic was the revealed holiness of God that many generations after it happened Jeremiah speaks of how God ". . . brought forth thy people Israel out of the land of Egypt with signs, and with wonders, and with a strong hand, and with a stretched out arm, *and with great terror*" (Jer. 32:21, emphasis added).

There were notable exceptions, of course, for Moses, after forty days in the mountain with God, seemed to become very comfortable in the presence of God's holiness, and David and Isaiah seemed to learn to relax in God's presence. But in most cases when men saw a demonstration of God's holy nature they reacted far more in fear than in faith. God was loved from a distance but was viewed with dread more than desire to approach him.

But this was exactly the opposite of what God desired. From the creation of Adam, God has yearned for intimate, interpersonal fellowship with men. He did not want to drive them off, He sought to draw them near, but the gulf between them proved to be too wide. The disparity between the two natures was too great. Men could not respond comfortably to God.

But God had a plan. Paul summarizes it in writing: "But when the fulness of the time was come, God sent forth his Son, made of a woman, made under the law, To redeem them that were under the law, that we might receive the adoption of sons. And because ye are sons, God hath sent forth the Spirit of his Son into your hearts, crying, Abba, Father. Wherefore thou art no more a servant, but a son; and if a son, then an heir of God through Christ" (Gal. 4:4-7). God's plan was to change us from what we are into what He is. He purposed to make us to become full sons and joint-heirs with Jesus Christ (Rom. 8:17).

Holiness Brought Through Christ Jesus

The implementing of this plan required the sending of Jesus to demonstrate God's holiness on a level that man could accept, and the imparting of the Holy Spirit into the believers to change their natures.

Christ, the Holy One, was separated from heaven to fulfill a mission on earth on behalf of the triune God. God desired to restore man to the holiness he had lost through sin, thereby making it possible for man to return to fellowship with a holy God. It was totally impossible for man to achieve this on his own, for in his unholiness he could not even conceive of true holiness. In his fallen state there was no way he could achieve it even if he did perceive it, and furthermore, in his separation from God he could not receive it if God had offered it to him. So it became necessary for God to bring a demonstration of holiness to awaken an awareness of it and to stimulate a strong desire for it. What man could not do for himself, God did for him. He did not come as a theophanic manifestation (God in angel form), but He became a man without losing the reality of being God. This was necessary in order for him to take our place at Calvary. Angels cannot die; only man is under the sentence of death, so to redeem us from death Christ had to become what we are in order to die our death for us.

Furthermore, he was "made under the law" (Gal. 4:4). He did not come as a lawgiver, but as a fulfiller of the law. Holiness could not come by giving man a new code, or else Moses would have brought holiness to mankind, but holiness came when God sent a man to earth who could perfectly keep God's laws and then vicariously offer that righteousness to others. He came "under the law" to "fulfill the law" in order to "redeem us from the curse of the law."

The purpose of his coming is listed as twofold. First, it is "to redeem them that were under the law. . ." (Gal. 4:5). Christ came to buy back those who have been pawned to sin. As God sent Hosea to the slave market to buy back his wife from the slavery she fell into after abandoning her husband, so God commissioned Jesus to buy sinners off the slave auction block.

Second, Christ came ". . . that we might receive the adoption of sons" (Gal. 4:5). He not only redeemed—He restored! We were purchased not merely to become servants of God but to be sons of God. It is not merely workers God is seeking, but worshipers (John 4:24); but Christ must restore men to divine holiness before they can, "Worship the Lord in the beauty of holiness" (Ps. 29:2). And He has done just that! Since our relationship is authenticated, our worship response is assured. With the same Spirit that dwelt in Christ dwelling in us, "Abba Father" comes quite naturally.

That Christ's display of God's holiness was acceptable to men is self-evident in the Gospels, and is discussed in chapter three. That his purchase of our redemption was completed is attested throughout the epistles, and confirmed by the testimony of the disciples, the apostles, and thousands of saints through the ages.

That Christ succeeded in his mission to earth is incontestable. While men in general may not have seen the Father in Jesus, Peter did; the rest of the disciples eventually did; the centurion at the cross did; and his intimate followers, both men and women, did. Concluding the agonizing hours on the cross, Jesus cried out to the Father, "It is finished" (John 19:30). God's plan to display the power of holiness had succeeded, for the holiness in Jesus refuted the power of unholiness displayed in humanity. At that moment sin's power was broken, sin's control was canceled, sin's stain was cleansed, sin's penalty was revoked, sin's guilt was remitted to Christ, and sin's victims were allowed to share in Christ's victory to become partakers of the divine nature. What He was, we can now become, because of the finished work of the cross.

The scriptural terminology is, "Being justified freely by his grace through the redemption that is in Christ Jesus: Whom God hath set forth to be a propitiation[Gk. "mercy seat"] through faith in his blood, to declare his righteousness for the remission of sins that are past . . . To declare, I say, at this time his righteousness: that he might be just, and the justifier of him which believeth in Jesus" (Rom. 3:24-26).

In the New Testament the words justify, justification, righteous, righteousness, just, right, and meet are all translations of the same Greek root, *dikaioo*. While justification is basically a legal term signifying a declaration of rightness or innocence, it is easy for us to impose our American system of justice upon the Scriptures and come up with a concept of acquittal that is based upon unavailability of evidence, uncertainty of the law, or unaccountable mercy on the part of the judge. But divine justification is never the result of clever lawyer action, or of deals made in private chambers, and certainly we could never conceive of a situation where God's law was inadequate to cover the offense. Justification in the Bible sense is far more the act of God that removes the believing sinner's guilt and the penalty incurred by that guilt, and that bestows a positive righteousness.

In my book *Let Us Enjoy Forgiveness*, I write: "Justification relates to man's position, not his condition. It is basically a change in a man's relation or standing before God. Man . . . once under divine condemnation . . . is now the subject of divine commendation. According to the language of the Scriptures it means to declare, or cause to appear innocent or righteous. It is to reckon righteous, or not to impute iniquity. To justify is to set forth as righteous. . . . It does not deal directly with character or conduct, but with guilt and punishment. . . . Justification is securing a new reputation through Christ and being accounted righteous before God. It means far

41

more than acquittal, for the repentant sinner receives back in his pardon the full rights of citizenship."[7]

Furthermore, as Rev. Robert Baker Girdlestone says, ". . . the process of Divine acquittal is so blended with the entrance of spiritual life into the person acquitted, that, though they are theoretically distinct, one cannot be fully stated or even comprehended without reference to the other."[8]

So in being justified there is a removal of the guilt of sin, an answering to the penalty of sin, and an impartation of the divine life as an antidote to sin. We are freed, forgiven, and filled with God. Our past is canceled, our present is enriched, and our future is assured, all because we have been justified by his grace.

For so many years I thought that my justification depended upon my sanctification; that is, that my standing before God was dependent upon the holiness of my life. This kept me filled with insecurity and fear. Every little inconsistency in my life became a threat to my salvation. While denying that I could earn my salvation, I was, in practice, trying to deserve it. I felt that I needed to be worth sanctifying, unaware that I can only be made worthy of God's holiness.

I will never forget the camp meeting in which I requested a private conference with the morning Bible teacher to discuss his teaching on justification, for it did not fit my doctrinal concepts. He was quick to offer me time, but I never had to accept his gracious offer, for in parting he lovingly said, "Judson, remember that no matter what man has taught you, God has declared you justified because of the work of his Son at Calvary. You merely need to identify with his cross in faith."

Illumination came in that moment. Light pierced the darkness of my understanding and I saw, almost instantly, that my justification was totally dependent upon what Christ has already done for me; it is a declaration of my righteous standing before God by imputation and is not affected by my level of holiness. What peace flooded my soul that morning! I shall ever bless dear Brother Alan Banks for causing me to know that the work of Christ has been done for us and nothing we can do will add to that work or take anything from it.

It is Jesus who not only made it possible for us to be separated from the slavery of sin, but also separated unto the perfect will of God. We too can be holy! His price became our profit, for in enduring separation from God for a season Jesus opened an access to God for eternity. He did not compromise his holiness; He compassionately channeled it to the unholy. He did not defile God's holiness; He displayed and delivered it to men in such a way as to please the Father.

Holiness Brought Through The Spirit

God's love and his holiness made a way to rescue man from sin and to return him to holy living. God himself took the penalty of our sins at Calvary in order to release us from sin's penalty, power, pollution, and guilt, and to restore us to fellowship with a holy God. Only God is absolutely holy; all other holiness is derivative. We have a holy God on one extreme and unholy men on the other, with God's Son purchasing holiness for men at Calvary and God's Spirit effecting that holiness day by day in their lives. The entire work of relating redemption to sinners is vested in the Spirit of God. It is He who gently begins the process of making us aware of sin, and who so convicts us of its wrong that we begin to sorrow over, regret, and eventually repent of sin.

This process probably began in response to a sermon,

testimony, or exhortation given by a Christian who was endued with the power of the Holy Spirit. His words were etched indelibly into our consciences, and like fishhooks were so barbed that we could not extract them. Again and again the Spirit reminded us of what we had heard until our minds resounded like an echo chamber. When we turned to the radio or the television for relief we "accidentally" tuned in gospel preaching, and we heard the same words another time. If in desperation we turned to the Bible for solace, we read the words that were burning in our hearts until we could no longer stand the agony of conviction, and we cried out to God for forgiveness.

At that very point the Holy Spirit began to apply the provisions of Calvary and washed us from the stain of sin while informing us that we had been declared righteous—justified—in the presence of the Father. He also baptized us into Christ so that we became a member of the body of Christ and began to develop the fruit of the Spirit within our lives. What love, joy, and peace flooded our beings! It was like starting life all over again with the purity and innocence of a baby. We had truly been "born again" by the action of the Holy Spirit. He removed our unrighteousnesses, placing them on the cross of Christ Jesus, and then imparted God's righteouness deep within our spirit as a replacement for sin, thereby sharing some of God's holiness with one who had been an enemy of God.

In bringing holiness to the earth God proclaims us holy—that is, set apart unto himself and his service—while Jesus purchases our holiness at Calvary, and the Holy Spirit provides holiness in the day-by-day application to our lives.

In his work of sanctification, or holiness, the Holy Spirit exercises a two-fold ministry: one to the unsaved, another to the saved. The first is called positional sanctification and refers to the work of the Spirit in bringing a lost sinner to the act of faith in the Lord Jesus as Savior. The second is called progressive sanctification and speaks of the work of the Spirit in causing Christians to grow in the knowledge and likeness of the Lord Jesus.

God has imputed his righteousness to the obedient ones; Jesus has conferred his justification upon the repentant ones, and the Holy Spirit has implanted his holiness in the consecrated ones by making his personal abode in their spirits.

The work of the Father is in the heavens, and that of the Son is on the earth; but the Spirit works in the individual's life. By this chain of action heaven's holiness that once threatened men now transforms them.

As the song writer has put it, "Heaven came down and glory filled my soul."

CHAPTER FIVE

Holiness and Sanctification

In defining God's holiness as the consummate holiness, perfection, purity, and absolute sanctity of His nature, we recognize that He is entirely apart from all that is evil and from all that defiles, both in himself and in relation to all his creatures. There is absolutely nothing unholy in him at all, consequently there is nothing within him that can be sympathetic with defilement and sin. When Solomon declared, "The way of the wicked is an abomination unto the Lord," and "the thoughts of the wicked are an abomination to the Lord" (Prov. 15:9, 26), he was merely reechoing the fundamental manifestation of God's holiness—hatred of sin. God not only hates sin, He is its uncompromising foe. Sin is vile and detestable to God, and it has produced an infinite distance between God and the sinner. God was even forced to turn away from his only begotten Son when the sins of the world were vicariously laid upon him, for there is no tolerance for sin in God's nature because of his holiness.

In contrast to that, man is singularly sinful. "For all have sinned, and come short of the glory of God," the

Word declares (Rom. 3:23). This extreme cannot be ignored if God and man are to be reunited in fellowship. Nor can it adequately be bridged through a simple declaration of God that men are now justified. The two must share the same nature if there is to be intimate communion. "Can two walk together, except they be agreed?" the prophet asked (Amos 3:3).

Knowing that God will not change (Heb. 13:8) and that man cannot change himself (Matt. 6:27) the only hope of reconciliation comes in allowing God to change that man. If man will submit his will to God, God will set that man apart from sin unto God's service, and then the Spirit of God will begin to progressively change that man into the character of his God. This work is generally called "sanctification" in the Scripture, although that English word comes from the same Hebrew and Greek words which are translated "holiness."

Commenting on this, Rev. Girdlestone says, "Few religious words are more prominent in the Hebrew Scriptures than those which spring from the root *kadash*, which is used in some form or other to represent the being set apart for the work of God. Perhaps the English word sacred represents the idea more nearly than holy, which is the general rendering in the Authorized Version. The terms sanctification and holiness are now used so frequently to represent moral and spiritual qualities, that they hardly convey to the reader the idea of *position* or *relationship* as existing between God and some person or thing consecrated to Him; yet this appears to be the real meaning of the word."[9]

Rev. Girdlestone also points out that *kadash* applies to places, to times, and to persons, but that the point involved in every case is relation or contact with God. This helps us to realize that if God's demand to holiness seems excessive it is probably because we have forgotten how things come to be holy. The place of the burning bush is holy because God is there; the temple is holy because it is God's house; the prophet, because he is God's man. All holiness is *derived*; things and people are holy only as they are near Him who is holy. Holiness is always *given*—it is given by grace and received through faith—but it is given while the person is in near proximity to the holy God.

The Greek word that is the equivalent of the Hebrew word *kadash* is *hagiazo*. Both words are translated "holy" and "sanctification" with little discernable difference in the meaning of these two words. Of the fifteen passages in which the nouns denoting holiness or sanctification are used in the New Testament, there does not appear to be anything distinctive in the use of the words by the different writers. Each seems to view the word about the same way.

Kenneth S. Wuest, for some years the professor of Greek studies at the Moody Bible Institute, says, "The classical Greek word meaning *to sanctify* is *hagizo,* which means to *consecrate*, for instance, altars, sacrifices, *to set apart for the gods, to present, to offer.* The word used in the New Testament answering to *hagizo* is *hagiazo,* which means to place in a relation to God answering to His holiness! Neither word means merely 'to set apart,' but in the case of the pagan word, 'to set apart for the gods,' and in the case of the Christian word, 'to set apart for God.' "[10]

Enlarging somewhat on this thought, Dr. James Hastings, a scholar of the past century, wrote, "The characteristic New Testament word for *holy* is, as we have seen, *hagios.* . . . It is generally believed that the fundamental idea which underlies the word is that of separation, and that its moral signification therefore is: separation from sin, and so, consecration to God. The

Christian use of the word lifted it into accord with the highest ethical conceptions, and gave it the idea of separateness from the sinful world, harmony with God, the absolutely good Being, moral perfection. Thus, *hagios* is, above all things, a qualitative and ethical term. It refers chiefly to character, and lays emphasis upon the demands which that which is sacred in the highest sense makes upon conduct."[11]

He further says that, "*Hagios* expresses something higher than sacred; higher than outwardly associated with God; higher than reverent, pious, worthy, honourable, pure, or even free from defilement. *Hagios* is more positive, more comprehensive, more elevated, more purely ethical and spiritual. It is characteristically Godlikeness, and in the Christian system Godlikeness signifies completeness of life."[12]

Viewing *sanctification* as characteristically *godliness*, and that this signifies completeness of life, I better understood some of the Holiness people of my boyhood days who, in spite of what seemed to be a rather narrow life, enjoyed life to the fullest. By their experience of sanctification which brought them into the holiness of God they seemed to find more pleasure in a worship service than a pleasure seeker will ever find in places of amusement. They did not need the elixir of wine, nor the stimulation of drugs to "free them"; instead, they allowed the divine nature of God to come into their lives in such a way that they had no need to escape; they genuinely enjoyed life.

Oswald Chambers seemed to feel that sanctification of the Spirit will be evidenced in the individual believer's daily walk for he wrote, "Holiness means unsullied walking with the feet, unsullied talking with the tongue, unsullied thinking with the mind—every detail of the life under the scrutiny of God. Holiness is not only what God gives me, but what I manifest that God has given me."[13] As Moses still glowed with the light of God on his face when he came down from the mount (Exod. 34:29-35), so we should manifest the holiness of God when we come out from being in his presence. It should affect our whole attitude towards life.

Benjamin Hellier used to insist that "in the New Testament the only Christian life *allowable* is that of entire sanctification. For those who are stopping short of this there are exhortations, warnings, expostulations, invitations, prayers; but the life there presented to every believer is one of a surrendered will, an obedient heart, a victorious Spirit-filled life in union with Christ, bringing salvation from sin, and leading to steady growth, through increasing knowledge and manifold temptation. This is the true answer to those who ask where the New Testament speaks of a second blessing. Salvation is *one* blessing, which many Christians, through their own fault or that of their teacher, are not receiving in its completeness."[14]

If Mr. Hellier is right, then a lot of Christians, including myself, must have stopped short of what is available to them, for I have observed much struggling with sin, carnality, passions, pride, and controlling habits in the church. As a matter of fact, it is only in the church that I see much struggling with these things, for in the world these are the ruling forces of life.

Perhaps this is because until a man is born again he does not see another way of life. We are all such prisoners of our environment that until we see something different as available to us, we will continue to function the way we have been trained to function. The man who has never known anything but lust is not capable of moving out of it into love any more than the man born in the jungles of the Amazon is capable of living in New York City. For all of them there must come an experience outside of themselves that will broaden their capacity to understand and transport them from one culture to another. This is what sanctifying grace does for us: it enlarges our concepts and enables our spirit to move to the higher realm.

In Romans 5 Paul declares that sin entered (v. 12), sin abounded (v. 20), and sin reigned (v. 21); but in Romans 6:13 he urges us to "yield yourselves unto God . . . and your members as instruments of righteousness unto God." We must overcome not only the entering and abounding of sin in our lives, we must also overcome its reign. Personally, it seems less to be sin at the helm; it usually is self. But the exercise of the self-will against the divine will of God is the surest essence of sin. This is what caused Lucifer's expulsion from heaven.

I discovered that God's sanctification needed to work outward through the areas of my life more closely bound up with my sensuous nature and my false egoism. I found myself the possessor of many faculties that were not yet adjusted to God's ends, but were often singularly biased toward my own ends. "I," "me," and "my" were the dominant forces in my life.

Sanctified Body

Paul writes, "I pray God your whole spirit and soul and body be preserved blameless unto the coming of our Lord Jesus Christ" (1 Thess. 5:23). Sanctification is a work of God through the Holy Spirit that affects the entire nature of man, including the body, for the body is the instrument of our higher nature and functions as the slave or servant for our soul and spirit. But the body has its own appetites and cravings which are capable of being perverted through excess, indulgence, and lethargy. Furthermore, the body which is designed to serve the soul and spirit sometimes seeks to become their master. Physical cravings can be allowed to override spiritual longings. Gluttony, sexual wantonness, and drunkenness (which are simply perversions of God-given physical appetites) have kept people from relating to God both in Bible and modern times.

Paul said, "I keep under my body, and bring it into subjection . . ." (1 Cor. 9:27). He had just described the discipline that the athletes in the stadium put their bodies through, and said that he would equally discipline his body for the sake of preaching the gospel. The body is not to be ignored or despised, merely regulated. It is the apex of all of God's earthly creation. The Psalmist said, "I will praise thee; for I am fearfully and wonderfully made: marvellous are thy works" (Ps. 139:14). Not only that, God has designs for the use of our bodies. "What?" Paul asks, "know ye not that your body is the temple of the Holy Ghost which is in you?" (1 Cor. 6:19). "If any man defile the temple of God, him shall God destroy; for the temple of God is holy, which temple ye are," he adds (1 Cor. 3:17).

Sanctified Soul

The soul—seat of our affections and desires—is the connecting link between our spirit and the world in which we live. If the body is the seat of self-consciousness then the soul becomes the seat of world consciousness. Here are the intellect and emotions of life. In man's soul are capacities to respond to life, to appropriate life, and to effect changes in the person's behavior because of these soulish responses. Watch what happens to people when music is played, for an example.

But this sensitive area of life is easily perverted to covetousness, lust, anger, and the many other soul passions that corrupt and embitter society. The mind is tempted to be alienated from God (Eph. 4:18) instead of being aligned with him. Jesus taught that even if we keep our body from doing wrong it is not righteousness in God's sight unless our desires are as pure as our behavior. For instance, not venting anger is not to be equated with not having anger, and never committing adultery physically is not moral purity if we do it in our soul.

Oh, the appetites in the soul! Hunger for beauty, longings for music, cravings for fellowship, thirstings for intellectual attainments that should draw us to Christ Jesus are often satiated in something earthly. These cravings are often as difficult to bring under control as the physical appetites. The soul, too, must be sanctified if we are to walk in divine holiness.

Sanctified Spirit

It is man's spirit that connects him with the divine and invisible world, but man's spirit is prone to pride and unbelief, and so quickly opens to the condemnation of the devil. Personally, I found my spirit to be a very weak and vacillating faculty that was often forced into a tug of war with my body and soul. How seldom it won the struggle! The highest part of my being that was meant to rule my whole nature often found itself being ruled by my baser nature and imprisoned by the emotions of my soul. Instead of being allowed to soar heavenward to God, it was often hitched to the wagon of religious endeavor and made to do slave labor. Although my spirit had been set free from the bondage of sin, it was not yet released from the bondages of my lower nature. My spirit was not in control of me; I was in control of it.

Then the Lord quickened the first part of 1 Thessalonians 5:23 to me: "And the very God of peace sanctify you wholly; and I pray God your whole spirit and soul and body be preserved blameless unto the coming of our Lord Jesus Christ." With the red-hot branding iron of his Spirit, God burned the words "sanctify you wholly" into my mind. In the preceding verses the apostle had exhorted the Thessalonians as to what *they* were to do: rejoice, pray, give thanks, quench not the Spirit, etc. Then suddenly he turned from the work of the human will to the work of the divine Spirit, and said, "The very God of peace himself sanctify you wholly." When we do what we can do, God will do for us what we cannot do. And it will be done by the God of peace, not the God of war. When we finally learn that all of our struggles with self are to no avail and submit ourselves to the God of peace for his changings, his calmness and peace replace our conflicts and pressure. It was the power of that peace that gave Paul the strength to control the temptations which assailed his vehement, sarcastic, fiery soul, to bear the burdens of the weak, and to submit silently to the slanders and scorns of the church and the world. Likewise, we need that divine peace to bring our whole being under the control of the Holy Spirit.

If sanctification is to be done by God it will have to begin in that point of our life that touches God—our spirit. We need to stop focusing on the wrong desires of our souls and the improper appetites of our bodies and specialize in getting our spirits in contact with God on a regular basis.

When I changed from the negative to the positive approach, amazing transformations began to take place in me on a gradual but continuing basis! I began to realize that my reason was becoming filled with the all-pervasive presence of God. I was not having to consciously think of God; his presence was with me continually. I also noticed that the faculty of my mind was not only cleansed from defilement but began to reflect the mind of God. Regularly I found myself not only meditating on God but thinking his thoughts and filled with his wisdom and knowledge. I found that my mind was beginning to comprehend the Word of God, and that where study of the Bible had been a laborious task, it was becoming a pleasant experience. It seemed that a veil was lifted from my eyes, and I could see and comprehend spiritual things that had been only shadows before. I discovered insight to the Scriptures that was not based on comparing verse with verse or having a knowledge of the original languages. With the opening of my spirit to God came an opening of my understanding of the ways and Word of God. It was a whole new world to me.

The sanctification of the soul, with its affections and desires, passions and appetites, follows the sanctification of the spirit. When our spirit is brought into a right relationship with God it becomes the controlling force in our life; our ego takes residence in the spirit, and our soul begins to receive orders from our spirit instead of giving orders to that spirit. We find a new channel of love that brings healing and gives direction to all the emotions of our soul. Some call this a "baptism of love," and the term is aptly expressive even if it is not scripturally accurate. As the Spirit of God is allowed to work in our soul level, we will find that our soul's desires become holy, its passions clean, its thoughts pure, its impulses godward, and that its delight will be in the will of the Lord. The tugging of the old nature with its evil lusts will be over. A new life · comes!

Naturally this requires much cooperation on our part

and some pain and many tears, for all of us dread and fear change. But God has begun a work in the spirit that cannot be completed until the soul knows his sanctifying power.

Since it is not in its own strength and beauty that the glory of the body consists, but in its connection with the other parts of man, bringing our body into the sanctifying work of the Spirit will prove to be the easiest of all. The body is the servant of man's higher nature and the avenue of communication between it and the outer world, so when the higher nature is brought into an intimate relationship with God the body begins to reflect it to the world.

We need to realize that if the spirit be preserved it will tend to preserve the soul, and if the soul be preserved, it will tend to preserve the body. God begins his work with man's conscience and reason, then descends to his social affections and desires, and then governs and regulates man's bodily appetites. What the apostle prayed for is that every man's spirit should be as much in communion with God as the spirit of Jesus Christ; his soul as full of social affection and unselfish desire; his body as much the pure and willing instrument of his superior nature in God's service as was Christ's. Then he would be sanctified wholly. All the parts of his being, like the strings of a piano, would vibrate in perfect unison with each other at the touch of the master's hand.

Is this achievable? I think so, for it is not man sanctifying himself but the God of peace sanctifying him. It is the divine Spirit of the unseen Christ breathing into man's spirit good desires, pure motives, and lofty inspirations, instilling steady belief in a better world, and giving a quiet assurance of a blessed hope hereafter. It is the work of the Holy Spirit shedding meekness, gentleness, purity, and love. It is man's higher nature being filled with love, joy, and peace, and his lower nature being filled with gentleness, goodness, and temperance.

W.E. Evans reminds us that the word "wholly" in Paul's prayer "and the very God of peace himself sanctify you wholly" (1 Thess. 5:23) means complete in every part and perfect in every respect, whether it refers to the Church as a whole or to the individual believer. Someday the believer is to be complete in all departments of Christian character, no Christian grace missing. He will be complete in the spirit, which links him with heaven; in the body, which links him with earth; and in the soul, as being that on which heaven and earth play. He will have maturity in each separate element of Christian character: body, soul and spirit.

Oswald Chambers puts it, "By sanctification the Son of God is formed in me; then I have to transform my natural life into a spiritual life by obedience to Him. . . . I have the responsibility of keeping my spirit in agreement with His Spirit, and by degrees Jesus lifts me up to where He lived—in perfect consecration to His Father's will, paying no attention to any other thing.[15]

How the Spirit has sought to teach that principle to us. We run the risk of being carnally minded if we don't, and a worldly state of mind and spirit limits the range of our faculties and finally destroys them, while it dissolves the harmony which God has established between us and all things around us—or, in a word, sin robs life of its promise. A godly state of mind secures the promise, makes life joyful, and cements the harmony of souls. Godliness is to a man's spirit, even in this life, what the warm, bright air of a summer morning is to the birds and flowers. This is the atmosphere in which they can most freely expand themselves, which moves and tunes their songs of praise. We know what the glow of health is in the body, but to enjoy this life truly, there must also be a glow in the soul. Godliness sets the vivid blood rushing through its channels and makes every act and utterance musical with joy. How imperative it is, then, that we be "wholly" sanctified.

Learning to Live in Two Worlds

As the life of Christ is formed in our spirit, affecting our soul and body, we touch God's kingdom more and more frequently. Times of prayer cease being times of petition and command and become times of adoration and communion. We find fellowship with God that we had only read about before. Our spiritual understanding opens to know and to participate in things that were totally unknown to us before. We begin discovering a totally different world—God's world. Its beauties beckon us, its music allures us, its magnitude challenges us, and our citizenship invites us to participate in it.

But we are earthy, living in a fleshly body with natural demands upon our time and energies. Still, we touched God's world and found ourselves struggling to live in the spirit so that we could enjoy the benefits and blessings of that supernatural realm.

We soon discover that resisting evil and struggling with our ego is not the only conflict to be found in sanctification. At times we feel like we are literally being torn apart. Our loyalties are divided, and our desires divergent. We are torn between two loves, not really wanting to give up one for the other, but desperately trying to combine the best of both worlds. At times the conflict gets so severe that we cannot enjoy either world; we are miserable in life and miserable in the spirit. We frequently condemn ourselves for our vacillation of love and compare ourselves to a bigamist. We simply have not yet learned to live victoriously in both worlds. But it is not a choice of either/or; it is both/and.

LET US BE HOLY

During the many years that I pastored in Oregon I was within a two-hour drive of the renowned sea lion caves where the largest species of seals used to congregate during the mating season. I always enjoyed watching them both in the water and on the rocks, for I seemed to be able to identify with them in at least one aspect: they, too, struggle to live in two worlds simultaneously. They are air-breathing mammals that come to land to breed and bear their young, but they are far more at home in the water than they are on the land. As swimmers they are graceful, playful, and powerful, but on the land they are lumbering, clumsy, and painfully awkward. Sometimes it seems that they are neither mammal nor fish, but some miserable concoction put together by a compromising committee.

Although they are masterful swimmers, it is not inherent in their nature. The *Encyclopaedia Britannica*, 1963 edition, declares that "seals are taught to swim by their parents." Born on the rocks, but destined to live in the sea, they must learn how to live in a world so different from the one into which they were born.

I relate to that, for although I was born into the natural world I was destined to live in the spiritual world. My time on the land is short; my full life will be lived in the sea of God's kingdom. But I was not born with an inherent ability to relate to or respond in that world. I have to be taught. Everything in God's world is foreign to me. Even though I may possess strong desires for holiness, I lack any innate ability to produce that holiness. I must remain on the rock until someone teaches me how to swim. That has become the work of the blessed Holy Spirit. He gently leads me from my natural world to his supernatural world. When He first encourages me to lumber across the rocks into the water, I feel more at home in my awkwardness than in his ocean of love, for I have not yet learned to swim. But I shall learn! I will learn how to be in this world but not of it. I will learn "how to possess[my] vessel in sanctification and honour" (1 Thess. 4:4). I will learn freedom in God's presence and will skillfully launch out into the ocean of his pleasures.

But it won't be learned in one easy lesson, and it will not be without a struggle. Sanctification has moved us off the rocks to which we were born into the ocean for which we were prepared, but the transition is a struggle both ways. After swimming so effortlessly it is painful to come up on the rocks again, but our mammal nature requires it.

St. Francis de Sales wrote, ". . . we must submit patiently to the trial of having a human, rather than an angelic nature." Surely, then, we can also submit patiently to the trial of having both a human nature and a divine nature at work at the same time. We can learn to live in two worlds simultaneously, for the spiritual life is the life of Christ being lived within us, and it becomes the overriding control of our natures in both worlds.

Sanctification does not make us a dual personality; it makes us a complete person able to cope with living in two different worlds without losing honesty, integrity, or reality. We may have our heads in the clouds and our feet on the earth, but we have received ". . . the grace of God that bringeth salvation . . . Teaching us that, denying ungodliness and worldly lusts, we should live soberly, righteously, and godly, in this present world: Looking for that blessed hope, and the glorious appearing of the great God and our Saviour Jesus Christ: Who gave himself for us, that he might redeem us from all iniquity, and purify unto himself a peculiar people, zealous of good works" (Titus 2:11-14). We live here, but look there.

But, of course, this has its times of conflict and struggle.

CHAPTER SIX

Holiness and Conflict

It is self-evident that one cannot become a saint in his sleep. Holiness must be the object of his pursuit. The lazy man will not be the holy man, for sanctification is brought about in the life of the believer by his separating himself deliberately from all that is unclean and unholy, and by presenting, continually and constantly, the members of his body as holy instruments unto God for the accomplishment of his holy purposes. By these individual acts of surrender unto holiness, sanctification soon becomes the habit of life.

Nonetheless, men naturally are more pleased in gratifying their bodily appetites and the selfish inclinations of their own hearts than in learning and doing the will of God, thus showing that they are opposed to holiness, in love with sin, and heirs of divine wrath. Unholy men have become content with their unholiness, but holy men have entered into combat with it.

Conflict with Concepts
Our beginning battles are less with sin and Satan than

they are with our own intellectual concepts, for as long as we are confused about the doctrine of sanctification anything we do will be confused. "If the army bugler doesn't play the right notes, how will the soldiers know that they are being called to battle?" Paul asks (1 Cor. 14:8, TLB). As long as we are confused about the doctrine of sanctification and our responsibilities in it, all signals given to the spirit and soul will be confusing.

Paul declares that the divine weapons issued to us for combat are mental weapons. "For the weapons of our warfare are not physical, but they are powerful with God's help for the tearing down of fortresses, inasmuch as we tear down *reasonings* and every proud barrier that is raised up against the *knowledge of God* and lead *every thought* into subjection to Christ" (2 Cor. 10:4, 5; Berkeley, emphasis added). We need divine power to get our minds straightened out to truly understand the Word of God and its provisions.

Confused Concepts of Sanctification

In striving for divine holiness many of our former concepts have to be unmasked as wrong. Those of us who were raised to "sanctify yourselves. . ." (1 Chron. 15:12) have had to learn that sanctification is not done by us nor for us; it is done *in* us. Still, "we are laborers together with God" (1 Cor. 3:9), so there is, obviously, a human element involved in our sanctification. We must find the balance of God providing and man participating.

One of the prominent confusions in the doctrine of sanctification is understanding the relationship of *positional versus progressive sanctification.* Keeping these properly balanced is not entirely easy, for too often we are only taught one or the other. But the Scriptures teach both positions and balances them like the two wings of a bird.

Theologically we understand that God the Father provides sanctification and we the recipients must practice it, and yet experientially we have often vacillated between trying to appropriate sanctification as an instantaneous act and accepting it as a progressive work. Our desires call for the former, while our deeds demand the latter. Sometimes in seeing God, by his own free choice and predetermined will, set us aside to holiness, we seek to accept his declaration that "ye are holy unto me" as final, but we fail to realize the light years of distance between our position in Christ and our condition in life. In being chosen to be his son we are positioned as a child of God, bearing his name and the benefits of his parentage. Yet we still live in this world, in the flesh, and are encumbered with our old nature. We do not realize that the nature of God comes as a seed that must be tenderly cultivated into a mature plant whose fruit is identical with the seed that entered the soil. God's declaration positioned us as "holy ones," saints, but it takes a continued and progressive manifestation of the Spirit of God within us to make our condition match our position. This is the progressive aspect of sanctification: causing our state in life to match our standing before God.

Oftentimes we fail to reconcile the facts that our sanctification is *both* positional and progressive. God's provision, and our entry into that provision, is an instantaneous work of grace, but the Holy Spirit's application and our acceptance of his work are very progressive. David expressed it, "Blessed be the Lord, who *daily* loadeth us with benefits" (Ps. 68:19, emphasis added); Jesus told his disciples, "If any man will come after me, let him deny himself, and take up his cross *daily*, and follow me" (Luke 9:23, emphasis added); while Paul testified, "I die *daily*" (1 Cor. 15:31, emphasis added). Being brought into the image of God is a *daily* activity. God loads us with the blessings of his nature; Christ brings us to his cross; and we identify with his death on a day-to-day basis. God gives us of his holiness, but we must more than receive; we must also relinquish our unholiness to make room for that divine image.

When we begin to see that God declares us holy, and the Spirit prepares us to become holy, just as the priesthood acquired a ceremonial holiness by consecration, we, too, become ceremonially holy by God's choice. But following the consecration ceremony, the priests had daily washings, sprinklings, sacrifices, and incense offerings in which to be involved. It was both positional and progressive for them, and it is for us as well. Sanctification is not a garment to be put on, but a spiritual principle to be lived; so that when even one portion of the manhood is affected by it, it passes into and affects the whole life. "If the root be holy, so are the branches" (Rom. 11:16).

The Bible's teaching on holiness and sanctification presents it as seed truth in the Old Testament, while the New Testament presents it as a developing plant. In the Old Testament, sanctification is an act of consecration that made the person or object holy, and he or it was considered separated unto God's service. But in the New Testament, sanctification is seen as a dynamic development of God's character in the consecrated one rather than mere separation unto God's service.

So sanctification is neither a simple act nor a process which must be completed before it can be strictly called by that name. It is complete at the outset in that we are set apart unto God, but it must grow and develop until God's very nature is worked into our entire life. Positionally, we are sanctified and declared to be holy by an act of God. Practically, we are sanctified by a work of God's Spirit inwardly, changing the sinner into increasingly perfect conformity to God's whole image.

One writer puts it, "Sanctification is a crisis with a view to a process—an act, which is instantaneous and which at the same time carries with it the idea of growth unto completion."

Paul seemed to understand this balance between what God has done for us and what He is doing in us, for he wrote, "I am crucified with Christ: nevertheless I live; yet not I, but Christ liveth in me: and the life which I now live in the flesh I live by the faith of the Son of God, who loved me, and gave himself for me" (Gal. 2:20). Paul saw a work done for him, with which he merely identified, and a work being done in him, in which he had to be an active participant. Holiness is not a mushroom growth; it is not the thing of an hour; but it grows as the coral reef grows: little by little, degree by degree. But it is coral while it is being built into a coral reef, and it is sanctification while it is developing into the holy nature of God.

Another area in which some Christians find themselves confused is in the area of *justification versus sanctification*. Some have so gloriously embraced justification that they do not see the need for anything further, while still others have only seen the sanctifying work of the Spirit and do not know how to appropriate the justifying work of Christ Jesus. W.E. Evans quite clearly defines the shades of difference between these two beautiful graces God has bestowed upon the believers. He writes, "If regeneration has to do with our nature, justification with our standing, and adoption with our position, then sanctification has to do with our character and conduct. In justification we are declared righteous in order that, in sanctification, we may become righteous. Justification is what God does for us, while sanctification is what God does in us. Justification puts us into a right relationship with God, while sanctification exhibits the fruit of that relationship—a life separated from a sinful world and dedicated unto God. . . . Sanctification may be viewed as past, present, and future; or instantaneous, progressive, and complete."[16]

False Concepts of Sanctification

Perhaps even worse than having to combat confused concepts of sanctification is coming to grips with false concepts. Often our search for divine holiness is greatly impeded by false concepts of sanctification. For instance, as long as we believe that sanctification is imputed we are not active participants in its production. We just wait for the right person to lay hands on us and to impute God's holiness into our natures. But while *holiness is imparted,* it is *not by imputation but by activation* of the divine life within us through the indwelling Spirit.

Some also stumble in *equating sanctification with glorification,* thereby putting the standard too high, always out of reach. But sanctification is not the final state of the saints in heaven; it is the required state of the saints on earth. We are not going to be sanctified; we are being sanctified right here and now. When Christ returns we will enter into full glorification, for "we shall be like him; for we shall see him as he is" (1 John 3:2). Until then, we are being brought into higher and higher realms of sanctification.

Falsely *equating sanctification with the repression of evil* is another erroneous view of sanctification we sometimes combat. Repression of evil is a virtue and is a

Christian grace expected of all saints, but it is not, of itself, sanctification. Repression of evil can be taught by the philosopher, practiced by the pagan, or preached in the Eastern cults and religions, but it does not produce the character of God in any of them. Sanctity, as an old divine once said, is "the life of God in man." The moralist knows nothing of it; he has neither the thing itself nor the word.

Equally dangerous is the view that *sanctification is the same as good works*. Sanctification is God's work in us whereby He imparts to our members a holy disposition, inwardly filling us with delight in his law and with repugnance to sin. But good works are acts of man which spring from this holy disposition. Sanctification is the source of good works, not the production of them. Sanctification imparts something to man; good works take something out of him, or, to put it another way, sanctification forces the root into the ground, and doing good works forces the fruit out of the fruitful tree. As I have already stated, holiness is the nature of God. Righteousness is the nature of God expressed, while sanctification is the nature of God worked in and out of human life.

But unquestionably the most damaging false view of sanctification is that *sanctification is sinless perfection*. Sinless perfection is the scarecrow that the devil uses to frighten God's children away from the finest grain in His fields. I have stumbled over hearing Christians testify to "entire sanctification" and then seeing some area of sin in their behavior. I had mentally equated sinlessness with sanctification. God has not promised us a sinless state here on this earth. As a matter of record, John wrote, "If we say that we have no sin, we deceive ourselves, and the truth is not in us. If we say that we have not sinned, we make him a liar, and his word is not in us" (1 John 1:8, 10).

We know that Satan cannot originate; he can only counterfeit what God has produced. Still, where there is counterfeit there is the real, and seldom is a valueless item counterfeited. It is absolute truth that God has offered us his holy nature and has imparted his Spirit to produce it within us, but it is gross error to declare that this will make us absolutely sinless, for there is no condition here upon the earth in which we do not need the atoning blood of Christ; there is no condition here in which we do not need the forgiveness of our trespasses; there is no circumstance here in which we do not need the perpetual intercession of our great high priest.

No, it is not sinless perfection but Christian perfection that God has set as our goal. Oswald Chambers said, "It is a snare to imagine that God wants to make us perfect specimens of what he can do; God's purpose is to make us one with Himself. The emphasis of holiness movements is apt to be that God is producing specimens of holiness to put in His museum. If you go off on this idea of personal holiness, the dead-set of your life will not be for God, but for what you call the manifestation of God in your life. . . . The thing that tells for God is not your relevant consistency to an idea of what a saint should be, but your real vital relation to Jesus Christ, and your abandonment to him. . . . Christian perfection is not, and never can be, human perfection. Christian perfection is the perfection of a relationship to God which shows itself amid the irrelevancies of human life. . . . I am called to live in perfect relation to God so that my life produces a longing after God in other lives, not admiration for myself."[17]

Rather than sinlessness, holiness is wholeness—the whole of Christ in the whole life. It vanishes when you talk about it but becomes gloriously conspicuous when you live it. A truly holy life has a voice that speaks when the tongue is silent, and is either a constant attraction or a perpetual reproof to the hearer.

Conflict in Combat

But even if we could get our doctrine straightened out perfectly it would not end the conflict, for there are still the flesh and the devil to contend with. We need to constantly balance our concepts between the finished work of sanctification and the unfinished work, for God's part seems to be finalized; it is our part that is still under construction. Although we accept that sanctification is not to be equated with absolute sinlessness, we will find that the outworking of sanctification in our lives comes to grips with sin on a regular basis. We can identify with Paul when he wrote, ". . . our flesh had no rest, but we were troubled on every side; without were fightings, within were fears" (2 Cor. 7:5). We soon learn that striving for holiness involves combat with sin.

But, then, I don't suppose we would need the Christian armor of God if there were to be no warfare. The fact that Paul urged the Ephesians to "take unto you the whole armour of God, that ye may be able to withstand in the evil day, and having done all, to stand" (Eph. 6:13) presupposes an enemy who is prepared for battle. Our defensive armament is listed as truth, righteousness, peace, faith, salvation and the Word of God. These are the weapons that will enable us to withstand evil in the day of its conflict with holiness.

Every step of sanctification into which the Spirit brings us will be challenged both without and within—by satanic evil and self-will. Each new conquest must be guarded until the enemy is convinced that we not only laid hold of sufficient divine energy to conquer the territory, but we have enough spiritual might to occupy and defend it. It was a happy day for me when I learned that once the devil is truly convinced that I will obey God in a specific area, he will back off and leave me alone. Until that point of surrender is complete and absolute, he attacks us repeatedly, hoping to cause us to give ground back to him. First Peter 5:9 tells us to "resist [Satan] stedfast in the faith," and James 4:7 assures us that if we "resist the devil . . . he will flee from you," but this does not mean verbal rebukings; it means standing in the full armor of God, committed to the will of God, and unswervingly committing our will to the will of God in the issue at hand.

It is not that our resisting of evil produces sanctification, but that the outworking of our sanctification resists evil. The more like God we become, the greater will be the resistance in our inner nature against sin in every form. Likewise, the more godliness we experience, the greater will be the outside pressure exerted against that nature, for Satan despises the holiness of God more than anything else in creation. Satan is far less concerned with the sinner's prayer than with the saint's submission to the sanctifying work of the Spirit, for this will forever separate the saint from Satan's dominion.

Oswald Chambers, in commenting on the promise given to "him that overcometh" (Rev. 2:7), wrote: "Life without war is impossible either in nature or in grace. The basis of physical, mental, moral, and spiritual life is antagonism. This is the open fact of life.

"Health is the balance between physical life and external nature, and it is maintained only by sufficient vitality on the inside against things on the outside. Everything outside my physical life is designed to put me to death. Things which keep me going when I am alive disintegrate me when I am dead. If I have enough fighting power, I produce the balance of health. The same is true of the mental life. If I want to maintain a vigorous mental life, I have to fight, and in that way the mental balance called thought is produced.

"Morally it is the same. Everything that does not partake of the nature of virtue is the enemy of virtue in me, and it depends on what moral calibre I have whether I overcome and produce virtue. Immediately I fight; I am moral in that particular. No man is virtuous because he cannot help it; virtue is acquired.

"And spiritually it is the same. Jesus said, 'In the world ye shall have tribulation,' i.e., everything that is not spiritual makes for my undoing, but 'be of good cheer; I have overcome the world.' I have to learn to score off the things that come against me, and in that way produce the balance of holiness; then it becomes a delight to meet opposition.

"Holiness is the balance between my disposition and the law of God as expressed in Jesus Christ."[18]

I could never get away from the fact that immediately following the great promises of "I will dwell in them, and walk in them; and I will be their God, and they shall be my people. . . . And will be a Father unto you . . ." (2 Cor. 6:16-18), Paul exhorts, "Having therefore these promises, dearly beloved, let us cleanse ourselves from all filthiness of the flesh and spirit, perfecting holiness in the fear of God" (2 Cor. 7:1). It is not all done for us; part of the process is done by us. We are responsible to resist evil. We must cleanse ourselves of all filthiness, and we are expected to perfect (not produce) holiness. What God puts within we must work out, even if that means conflict.

For me, this required resisting Satan; standing up to

temptation; refusing sin; and experiencing a continual cleansing of my heart and mind. I had struggled to do this for many years, but I had not found the balance of submitting myself to Christ when Satan came against me; of inviting Christ to meet the temptation for me; of embracing righteousness as a replacement for sin; and of the cleansing of my heart and mind with a fresh flow of the Word of God. Paul requires a cleansing from defilement to be coupled with "perfecting holiness in the fear of God." The first is an outgrowth of the second. If they do not function together we will end up in confusion, not holiness. Coming out of that confusion will require conflict, but that is merely part of the tension-release syndrome of learning to live a holy life. We will win this conflict and be "overcomers" if we will "fight the good fight of faith" (1 Tim. 6:12), because holiness is God's express will for man, and nothing short of man's refusal to enter the conflict is going to thwart God's will.

CHAPTER SEVEN

Holiness—God's Will for Man

Consistently in the Book of Revelation God is pictured as being surrounded by mighty living creatures, myriads of angels, martyrs, elders, and redeemed men, all of whom were made holy by God's will and action. Whether they are "holy angels," "holy prophets," or "holy men," God will always be surrounded by beings of his creation who share in his holiness. None others need apply for citizenship, for the Scriptures declare that holiness is that "without which no man shall see the Lord" (Heb. 12:14).

Howbeit, I am convinced that God still longs for the intimate companionship and fellowship He had with man before sin defiled his holiness and forced his expulsion from God's presence. No amount of holy angels can take the place man should have in the heavens. God is not angry with man; He long ago forgave him his sins. God simply will not and cannot have communion with a defiled saint. But He can, and will, cleanse him. Holiness and unholiness cannot fellowship together, for one of the prime manifestations of holiness is a hatred of sin. But while God cannot fellowship with or accept the unholy, He can and will share his holiness with anyone who strongly desires fellowship with him, for God passionately yearns to have this kind of communion with man. He certainly had it with the man Christ Jesus.

One of those times of intimate fellowship is recorded in John 17, which Spurgeon calls "the holy of holies of the Word of God."[19] It is truly the Lord's Prayer, for the portion we generally recite as "The Lord's Prayer" is actually a prayer the Lord gave for his disciples to pray; it is the disciple's prayer. But in John 17, Jesus, as our interceding high priest, enters the Holy of Holies of the heavens and speaks with the Father in close fellowship of love. Looking forward to his passion He asks that the Father would glorify him, thereby enabling the Son to glorify the Father (v. 1). Then He reports that He has completed his task on the earth, and glorified the Father in doing so (v. 4). In verse 9 He begins to pray for us that the Father would preserve us (v. 12), and that we might be filled with his joy (v. 13).

Then about midway in his prayer, Jesus pleads, "Sanctify them through thy truth: thy word is truth" (v. 17). Jesus specifically asks the Father to sanctify us in the same manner in which He had been sanctified (v. 19). Surely our holiness must be the will of the Father if Jesus prayed for its impartation to us, for He never prayed out of the will of God.

The theme of our Savior's great prayer of intercession was for our sanctification. "Sanctify them," He pleaded. He had already assured the Father that, "They are not of the world, even as I am not of the world," (v. 16), so his prayer was not for redemption or regeneration. He was asking the Father to complete something that had only begun during his ministry with the disciples. "Sanctify them."

Since the first meaning of "sanctification" is "set apart unto" it seems that Christ was petitioning the Father to set apart or dedicate the believers to divine service. Certainly that would be the meaning Christ had a little later in his prayer when He prayed, "for their sakes I sanctify myself, that they also might be sanctified through the truth" (v. 19), for Jesus was unblemished by sin, and his actions were unspotted, therefore He would never use "sanctify" concerning himself if He meant purification.

The prayer means, "Father, consecrate them to thine own self; let them be temples for thine indwelling, instruments for thy use." Remember how God set aside the entire tribe of Levi and ordained them to the service of the Lord, instead of the firstborn, and out of the tribe of Levi one family was taken and dedicated to the priesthood? Aaron and his sons are said to have been sanctified (Lev. 8:30). Later a certain tent was sanctified to the service of God, and it became a sanctuary. Everything used in that tabernacle from the altar to the ark, from the bowls to the snuffdishes, was declared sanctified (Num. 7:1). Because of this sanctification, none of these things could be used for any other purpose than the service of the Lord God. The fire, the bread, the oil, and the incense were all called holy and were reserved for sacred uses, under penalty of death for violation. These sanctified things were reserved for holy purposes, and any other use of them was strictly forbidden.

This is one part of the meaning of our Lord's prayer. He wants each of us to be consecrated unto the Lord, reserved and ordained for divine purposes. We do not belong to the world, it has no right or claim on our life any more. We do not belong to the devil, his authority over us was broken the moment we were given unto God. We do not even belong to ourselves to live under the dictates of a selfish will and stubborn pride. We are bought with a price, and we belong totally to the one who paid the price. We belong to Jesus, and He presents us to his Father, and begs him to accept us and sanctify us to his own purposes.

We cannot hire ourselves out to inferior objects, mercenary aims, or selfish ambitions; for we are now under solemn contract to God. We have lifted up our hand unto the Lord, and we cannot draw back. But who would want to draw back from such a covenant with God? It is both delightful and profitable to us, for although we belong to him exclusively it puts the complete responsibility for our lives in his hand. If there is a conflict, the battle is the Lord's. If there is a privation, the provision is the Lord's. If there is physical illness, the physician is the Lord, for the same covenant that makes us his makes him ours. It is the will of Jesus that the Father sanctify us to the service of God, thereby letting us know, and all the world know, that we are God's, because we belong to Christ.

But this prayer would suggest something additional, for those who belonged to God, and were dedicated to his service, were set apart and separated from others. There was a special service for the setting-apart of priests, and specific rites were performed even at the sanctifying of dedicated places and vessels. Everyone and everything that was separated unto the sacred was also separated from the profane; there could be no dual service. It was either all God's or it wasn't God's at all.

In his high priestly prayer Jesus asked the Father to separate those who were dedicated to him from the rest of mankind.

This is consistent with his ways throughout all of the

Bible. Abraham had to come out of Ur of the Chaldees, and Israel out of Egypt. Of his chosen the Lord said, "This people have I formed for myself; they shall shew forth my praise" (Isa. 43:21). In the New Testament the call is repeated: "Come out from among them, and be ye separate, saith the Lord, and touch not the unclean thing; and I will receive you, And will be a Father unto you, and ye shall be my sons and daughters, saith the Lord Almighty" (2 Cor. 6:17, 18).

Because this call has been misapplied, it is often ignored. Separation for separation's sake is not holiness. It is one thing to separate from the world, and another thing to be separate from the church. While we are taught to separate ourselves from believers who are in open and unconfessed sin, we err if we carry on this separation where it is not authorized by the Word of God.

It seems popular wherever a new touch of life is received to cry for all others to "come out from among them . . ." and join us. We are to be faithful to truth, but we are not to be of a contentious spirit, separating ourselves from those who are living members of the one indivisible body of Christ. To promote the unity of the church by creating new divisions is unhealthy. The churches in Corinth and Galatia were far from being perfect in life, and they had made many mistakes in doctrine, even on vital points, but since they were truly in Christ, Paul did not command any of the Christians to come out of those churches. Instead, he exhorted them to stand fast in Christ's liberty and urged them to come into a clearer knowledge of the true gospel.

But we cannot set aside the clear teaching of the Bible on being separated from the world, just because some have used it to their own ends, or have distorted it to authorize withdrawal from the mainstream of life. If the

Father sanctifies us unto his service, it automatically sanctifies us from the rest of mankind. The priests were never involved with the rest of Israel as they had been before their sanctification.

This being "set apart from" began before the foundation of the world when our names were written in heaven, and becomes a process in our lives beginning at our redemption and carries through the entire work of the Spirit within us. This separating work is commonly known as sanctification—a process by which the man of God is removed farther and farther from all fellowship with the unfruitful works of darkness, and is changed from glory unto glory, into an ever-growing likeness of his Lord, who was "holy, harmless, undefiled, separate from sinners" (Heb. 7:26).

These who are sanctified in this sense are no longer unequally yoked together with unbelievers (2 Cor. 6:14); they are not conformed to this present evil world (Rom. 12:2); they are strangers and pilgrims upon the earth (Heb. 11:13).

In every generation there have been those who think that the church would have a better ministry if she would learn the ways of the world, use her methods, and acquire her culture. They seem to feel that the world can be conquered by our conformity to it. But this is as diametrically opposed to the Scripture as light is to darkness. It will be a black day when the sun itself is turned into darkness, and it will be a sinful day when the church is turned into the world. When the salt loses its savor, and no longer opposes putrefaction, the world will rot with a vengeance. The seed of the woman knows no terms with the serpent brood but continual war.

Friendship with the world is impossible to one who has been sanctified, for Jesus said, "Ye are not of the world, but I have chosen you out of the world, therefore the world hateth you" (John 15:19). James warns us, "Ye adulterers and adulteresses, know ye not that the friendship of the world is enmity with God? whosoever therefore will be a friend of the world is the enemy of God" (James 4:4). The heart which has been given to Christ and purity must not wander forth to woo the defiled and polluted things of this present evil world. Separation from the world, not union with it, is Christ's prayer for us.

But the concept of separation cannot completely satisfy the depth of meaning Christ had in his prayer to the Father, for "sanctification" also means to make the people of God holy. "Sanctify them," that is, work in them a pure and holy character, is what the Lord prayed. Shouldn't we join the Lord in that prayer daily?

The Greek word used by our Lord is not the one that is rendered "purify," but it has another, a higher, shade of meaning than that. Had Jesus meant "purify" He would never have used the same word concerning himself two verses later. Jesus accepted that the disciples had come into the purifying work of God. We, too, must be purged from the common sins and ordinary transgressions of mankind, or else we are liars unto God, and deceivers of our own souls. If we are not moral, if we are not honest, if we are not kind, if we are not truthful, we are far from the kingdom. How could we be classified as children of God if we are not even decent children of men? The sin question must be settled at Calvary. There we are offered cleansing in the precious blood of Jesus (1 John 1:7).

But sanctification is something more than mere morality and respectability; it is not only deliverance from the common sins of men, but also from the hardness, deadness, and carnality of nature. Sanctification is deliverance from that which is of the flesh (even at its very best), and admittance into that which is spiritual and divine.

Our Lord prayed, "Father, spiritualize them; elevate them; make them to dwell in communion with thee; make them to know him whom flesh and blood cannot reveal or discern."

Sanctification is a higher word than purification, for it includes that word and vastly more. It is not sufficient to be negatively clean, we need to be adorned with all the virtues of the Spirit of God. If we are merely moral our righteousness does not exceed that of the scribes and Pharisees. If we pay our lawful debts, give alms to the poor, and observe the rites of our religion, we are not doing anything more than others whom we tend to consider as being in error.

Sanctification makes it possible for the children of God to exhibit the love of God, be filled with zeal for his glory, and live generous, unselfish lives. It enables us to walk with God, and commune with the Most High. Without sanctification we cannot enjoy the delicious sweets of our holy faith. The unsanctified are full of doubts and fears. They often say that the outward exercise of religion is a wearisome thing. And no wonder, for they do not know the internal joys of it, having never learned to delight themselves in God. Only those who walk in the light of the Lord's countenance can know the heaven on earth which comes of true godliness. This is what Jesus prayed the Father to do for us. "Sanctify them. . . ." And He ended his prayer with the petition, "Father, I will that they also, whom thou hast given me, be with me where I am; that they may behold my glory . . ." (John 17:24). Full sanctification is most essential to this, for will the unsanctified dwell with Christ in heaven? Will unholy eyes behold his glory? It cannot be. We cannot participate in the splendor and triumphs of the exalted Head if we are not members of his body, and certainly a holy head could not have impure and dishonest members. Uprightness of walk and cleanness of heart are absolutely requisite for the purposes of the Christian life, both here and in the hereafter. We must be holy, for Christ is holy.

In considering that holiness is God's will for man we do well to remember to whom this prayer is addressed. No one can sanctify a soul but Almighty God. He who made us must also make us holy, or we shall never attain that character. In directing his prayer, Jesus calls God "Holy Father." While it may be the mission of the holy God to create holiness, a holy *Father* can only be the Father of holy children, for like begets like. To those who believe in Jesus He gives power to become sons of God (John 1:12), and a part of that power lies in becoming holy according to the character of our Father who is in heaven. The very nature of God should encourage us in our prayers for holiness, for He yearns to work in us "both to will and to do of his good pleasure" (Phil. 2:13).

The tenor of this prayer urges us to realize that sanctification is a work of God from its earliest stage. We go astray by ourselves, but we never return to the great Shepherd apart from his divine drawing. Regeneration, in which sanctification begins, is totally the work of the Spirit of God. Subsequently, every thought of holiness, and every desire after purity, must come from the Lord alone, for we are by nature wedded to iniquity. Even so, the ultimate conquest of sin in us, and the making us perfectly like our Lord, must be entirely the work of the Lord God, who makes all things new, since we have no power to carry on so great a work of ourselves. We are only a creation—we cannot create!

"Sanctify them by thy truth, Father," was Christ's

plea. But the truth alone will not sanctify a man. We may maintain an orthodox creed, and it is proper and important that we do so, but if it does not touch our heart and influence our character what is the value of our orthodoxy? It is not the doctrine which of itself sanctifies, but the Father sanctifies by means of the doctrine.

We must learn to look out of ourselves and look wholly to God for this sanctifying work. We dare not try to work out sanctification by ourselves, as though we could perform it alone. We need to caution ourselves lest we imagine that holiness will necessarily follow because we have read the proper books, listened to the inspired tapes, or heard the anointed preacher. Even uniting in sacred worship will not, of itself, produce holiness. God himself must work within us; the Holy Spirit must live within us, and this comes as the result of our living faith in the Lord Jesus. We must believe in him for our sanctification just as we have believed in him for our pardon and justification. He alone can bestow sanctification upon us, for this is the gift of God through Jesus Christ our Lord.

It is God's will for man to be holy. God declared it, Christ prayed for it, and the Spirit applies it. When man's will matches God's will in this matter of sanctification the process begins in earnest.

But what God has willed for us—holiness—isn't synonomous with what we often call holiness—religious performance. If the second is the outgrowth of the first it can be beautiful, but if it is a substitute for the first it is a stench in the nostrils of God.

CHAPTER EIGHT

Holiness versus
Religious Performance

God has not only demonstrated the holiness of his character, but He has delegated that same holiness to his children. It is his will that we be holy, and it will take his power to effect it. Oswald Chambers says, "God has one destined end for mankind, viz., holiness. His one aim is the production of saints. God is not an eternal blessing-machine for men; He did not come to save men out of pity: He came to save men because He had created them to be holy."[20]

"Be ye holy; for I am holy" (1 Pet. 1:16). Although at times it seems like a completely unattainable goal, it is certainly an unquestionable command. God said it; that settles it!

There is no way of rationalizing away the command of this verse by examining the surrounding Scriptures, for the context begins by talking about the vision the early prophets had of the glory that was to come through Christ, and then urges us, "Brace up your minds for action, therefore, and be alert, and fix your hope fully on the grace that will be coming to you when Jesus Christ is revealed. As obedient children, do not shape your lives by the passions that controlled you in your previous ignorance; instead, as the One who called you is holy, so you yourselves should be holy in all your conduct; for it is written, 'You shall be holy, because I am holy' " (1 Pet. 1:13-16, Berkeley).

The verses that follow the text are as pointed as the ones that precede it. "Besides," Peter continues, "if you address Him as Father, who impartially judges according to each one's work, you need to behave reverently during the time of your exiles, well aware that you have been ransomed from your futile ways such as traditionally came down from your forefathers . . ." (1 Pet. 1:17, 18, Berkeley). Then he speaks of us purifying our souls; obeying the truth; loving the brethren from a pure heart; and of being born again. This doesn't leave any loopholes. God has determined that his children shall be holy.

This command to holiness that Peter writes is a direct quote from the Old Testament. Six times the Old Testament uses these very words, and a few other times the phraseology is different but the truth is the same. "Be ye holy, for I am holy."

The force of this verse is amplified when the context of Leviticus is read with it. In Leviticus 11:44, 45 this command is in the midst of the food laws that established what they could and could not eat. The basis of the food laws was neither that they would be strong nor that they would lose weight, but that they would be holy as God is holy.

In Leviticus 19:2 this command appears in the midst of a variety of laws: it precedes the commands concerning the keeping of the sabbath, relationships with parents, and abstaining from idolatry. They were not to go to church to get a blessing, but to be holy; nor were they to love their parents because it was "proper" but in order to be holy unto the Lord.

In Leviticus 20:7 the command sits between prohibition of any form of witchcraft and of uttering curses against the people. Each is unholiness in the sight of God.

In Leviticus 20:26 the command is amid the laws concerning separation of unclean animals from the clean, while in 21:8 it is in the regulations governing the marriage of the priests.

This matter of being holy, then, is far more than a deep religious feeling. It radically affects our life style. It is concerned with our attitudes, actions, associations, adoration, thoughts, love, obedience level, and even our marriage partner. Holiness is a governing principle of life to be manifested in every area of life as displayed inwardly and outwardly—towards God, ourself, or others.

But since we cannot behold the holiness of God without worshiping—at least no one in the Bible was able to refrain from worship when God manifested himself—holy people will want to express themselves in worship. They will seek out a body of believers to share the worship experience with them. What we are must be expressed, and if we are possessors of God's holiness we will want to express it in worship to God.

Because holiness and worship are so naturally interconnected it is easy to confusedly put one for the other. That is, if holiness will manifest itself in a worship response, then doesn't a worship response manifest holiness? Of course not. The Scriptures abound with illustrations of unholy men worshiping a holy God when his presence was made manifest. Balaam is a classic example of this. We too easily lose sight of which is the cause and which is the effect. When worship proceeds out of a holy life it will undoubtedly have certain rituals of expression, but duplicating those rituals will not produce the holiness.

For years people have performed prescribed patterns of religious behavior and convinced themselves that they were holy, but merely going to church and partaking of the sacraments cannot produce divine holiness. It might express it, but it cannot create it. Reading the Bible, singing in the choir, teaching in the Sunday school, or holding some church office absolutely cannot produce holiness, nor can it substitute for it.

Religious zeal, piety, sacrificial giving, and evangelical fervor are not holiness producers. God alone is the source of holiness, and only his Spirit can produce it in the life of the believer. Once produced it will express itself in any or all of these ways, but it is only an expression. How difficult it seems to be for some of us to learn this fundamental principle. Holiness is not produced *by* me, it is produced *in* me with my wholehearted cooperation. I wish I had known this many years ago.

Conversion Is Not Holiness

The Christian life is not merely a converted life—it is a holy life. Being born again is, indeed, the first step, but it certainly is not the final one. I had been soundly converted at the age of three. My parents attest to the definite change that occurred in my attitudes subsequent to that experience. Although I was very young, there is no question that Paul's declaration became my participation: "When someone becomes a Christian he becomes a brand new person inside. He is not the same any more. A new life has begun!" (2 Cor. 5:17, TLB). But I had not yet passed into the full holiness of God. I still had to be spanked for disobedience and disrespect. I had to be forced to obey some of the rules of the home, and taught proper relationships with my brothers and sister who subsequently came into the family. I was converted, but not completed. I had received new life but did not yet know how to release that life.

Through the years of my pastoring I have seen this story repeated many times. I have seen people converted from horrible lives of sin who thought that they were automatically holy because God had so supernaturally delivered them from unholy lives. But holiness is not merely the absence of the unholy. Holiness is a positive force seen in the moral nature of God himself, and while it is the power of holiness that releases us from the unholy thing, the mere absence of the unholy cannot produce holiness. Holiness is not a neutral zone, nor is it an automatic force that shows up when everything negative to it is removed. Essentially, holiness is the moral nature of God that man has been commanded to come into. "Be ye holy; for I am holy." Conversion is essential to holiness but does not, in itself, effect holiness. It is a beautiful beginning, but we need abundantly more.

Ceremony Is Not Holiness

Of course, at age three I wasn't concerned with holiness. My behavior was the responsibility of my parents. But as I matured in life and entered areas of ministry as a youth I searched for holiness with a fervor. I so wanted to live what I was preaching and singing to others. In listening to my father preach about the consecration of the Old Testament priests, I thought that I saw a ray of light which would guide me to personal holiness. I began to read everything I could find about the forms of worship that God instituted for those Old Testament believers. I read about the tabernacle with its priesthood, ordinances, ceremonies, and rituals, and I discovered that God had seemed to provide a "ceremonial holiness" for them. By the washing of water, anointing of blood and oil, and by the burning of incense these men were "set apart," "sanctified," "made holy." As long as they did what God had designated they were accepted as holy. This is it! I thought.

So I became very fervent in the rituals of our church. I became very active in the water baptismal services, sharing whatever part my father would grant me, whether as the song leader, the helper, or merely behind the scenes cleaning up after-the-fact. Oh, how I sought to release faith during those services. I identified with each candidate, yearning to receive something concrete in my own Christian experience. But I was never more holy after a baptismal service.

I also got involved in the Communion services. Usually my father would have me at the organ while the Communion was being served, and I would identify by faith with everything that was being done. My personal participation in the elements was with great zeal and anticipation. Surely this ordinance given to us by our Savior himself would make me holy. But it didn't—not in itself. In all my ministry as a pastor I sought to make the Communion service one of the most meaningful ordinances of the church, and we had some blessed services together. But I couldn't help noting that some who were very sincere and seemingly faith-filled when they partook got themselves embroiled in the miseries of sin before the week was over, so the ordinance of the Lord's Supper had not made them holy, either.

I was a very reverent and active participant in the sacrament of marriage and at the burial of the departed saints. I was active in all the forms of worship and rarely missed denominational functions. But I knew that I was not yet holy.

On repeated occasions I had hands laid on me, and great prayers were prayed over me. From time to time a word of prophecy came over me, and men of faith confirmed the call of God upon my life. But for all of this ceremony I was still unholy.

As my schooling ended and I was granted a license to preach, I thought this might be the final commission to holiness. But it wasn't. When I was consecrated to my first pastorate I was certain that this would be the ceremony that would induce holiness, but it didn't. Some years later, after my ministry had been proven in two pastorates, I was formally ordained to the ministry. This was a great highlight for me—a zenith toward which I had been striving for many years. When hands were laid on me I expected some great thunderbolt from heaven to pass through me, purging me once and for all from everything that was unholy and imparting the divine nature of holiness into my being. But it ended up as being more a case of empty hands being laid upon an empty head. The ceremony was completed, but little else transpired. Within the week I was aware of unholy attitudes and impure desires deep within me. There was still much of me that was unlike Christ Jesus.

I have always been somewhat of a freethinker, but I was quite faithful to the traditions of our fathers. I assumed that they knew what was best and that they had achieved holiness, so their pattern should be followed. But even doing things the way they had always been done did not satisfy my inner thirst for divine righteousness—for the holiness of God. I finally had to admit that although ordinances, ceremonies, and traditions surely have their place in the worship of the church, they are not capable of producing the divine image of God in our lives.

The Old Testament officers may have been called holy by ceremony but they had not yet conformed to the holiness of God's character. They were declared holy, just as we are declared righteous through justification by faith, but they were not yet prepared to manifest the holiness of the divine nature. Theirs was a positional holiness, not a personal holiness. I wanted more than positional holiness, for I had that by virtue of my office as pastor and by virtue of my ordination to the ministry. What I lacked was the personal involvement with God's holy nature.

Conformity Is Not Holiness

I had still another road to travel before I would believe that it was a dead end; it was called "conformity." Having been taught that the essential thing for holiness of life is to have a standard and then to live by that standard without deviation, I joined Paul in being a keeper of the law. I strictly observed the dress code of our church (with one notable exception during my last days at high school when I got a good buy on a pair of two-toned brown shoes that had faded in the window of the store where I worked—my father had considerable difficulty with his church board when I showed up on the platform in those "worldly" shoes). I stayed away from worldly amusements, with an occasional "backsliding" to attend a circus. My language was pure and without oaths, and my morals were perfect. I read the Bible through every year, prayed daily, witnessed to sinners regularly, attended all of the church services, visited the rest homes, preached on the street corners, and so forth. If a new rule for conduct of life was made, I memorized it and then implemented it in my behavior. I talked like our group, walked like them, acted and reacted as they did. But I did not have inner holiness, only outward conformity. I had learned how to be like them, but it is being like Christ that makes a man holy. This I had not yet learned.

Even conforming to the Word of God did not bring holiness. I became a good legalist and lived by the "letter of the law." But while I would not say it, I would think it. I certainly wouldn't do it, but I desired to do it. My actions were harmonious with the Word of God, but my attitudes weren't. Often, though my manifestations were holy, my motives were most unholy. For instance, I did not desire to be "good for nothing," so I managed to call attention to my goodness. While I did not achieve the praises of God, I seldom lacked for the praises of men. I became very proficient in doing the right thing for the wrong reasons. And I was miserable within, for I knew that the holiness others thought they saw in me was little more than an outward facade. Behind that false mask lived a man full of carnal desires and fleshly passions. I was involved in all of the right deeds and was making all of the correct declarations, but it was not producing the inner moral character of God. I still wasn't holy.

Cloister Does Not Produce Holiness

Coupled with my conforming to the standards that had been set by others was a feeling that I should cloister, or withdraw, myself from most of life. Perhaps, I felt, my answer to unholiness would be to separate myself physically from everything that even seemed to have a taint of sin in or upon it. Not only did I withdraw from active participation in the life of the community, but I withdrew from most people. I spent long hours secreted in my study, buried in books and the Bible. I did very little visitation even among the members of my own congregation. I was not involved in any community projects and felt that all service clubs were exceedingly sinful. I did not participate in sports, I did not make room for recreation in my life, and I was about as "anti-party" as a pastor could be. Even my family suffered from my withdrawal, for I found myself closeted in from even them much of the time.

There is no questioning the fact that God made good to come of the time spent alone with him and with books, and I was probably spared some wounds and hurts by my withdrawal from all but my little church world. But the motivation for the withdrawal was totally wrong. I was hiding from sin and sinners, fearing that I might catch something. I acted as though I had no immunity to disease and therefore created an artificial incubator in which to survive. And survive I did, but the isolation did not produce holiness—only a "holier-than-thou" attitude and a tendency to be introverted.

In all fairness I must admit I have met some very holy people who have literally cloistered themselves in a religious order or monastery, and I have also met some very frustrated people who have done the same thing. All have withdrawn from secular life, but not all achieved holiness. It is not the seclusion that produces holiness; it is Christ.

Consecration Does Not Produce Holiness

Since consecrating your life was the "in" thing to do in the circles of my younger Christian experience, I consecrated myself to the Lord, fully determined to live a consecrated life. Oh, how often I have stood before the altar of the church with my hands raised toward heaven while tears streamed down my face, singing, "Consecrate me now to Thy service, Lord, by the power of grace divine; Let my soul look up with a steadfast hope, and my will be lost in Thine."[21] It was moving, it was honest, and it was effective. It kept me pliable and pointed toward the Master's use. My consecrations varied as the altar calls differed. I consecrated myself to be a faithful witness in the school, and I was. I consecrated myself to be a servant to the saints, and served as janitor for two churches simultaneously. I consecrated myself to preach the gospel, and faithfully preached on the street corners, jails, missions, youth groups and in any church that would give me the opportunity. I consecrated myself to the mission field and would reconsecrate this dedication every time there was a missionary service. As much as I understood consecration, I was consecrated to God. But I still wasn't holy. In fact, the more I heard my father preach the gospel, the greater my intense resentment because it revealed that I was unholy. But it also awakened an intense craving for holiness. I responded to many of his altar calls as though I were a lost sinner needing salvation, when actually I was a consecrated saint desperately needing divine holiness.

Slowly I came to the conclusion that my life would not truly be a Christian life at all unless it was Christ's life living God's nature within me. I came to believe that holiness was not something I could achieve through conversion or consecration, much less by good works, but must be something I could receive through faith in Jesus Christ.

But while I had seen part of the truth, I still did not have a grasp on the whole, for I later learned that holiness is not only what God gives me, but what I manifest that God has given to me. I had to realize that holiness was neither I alone, nor Christ alone, but Christ giving, and me living. What I received had to be released; what I had accepted from his life had to be applied to my life.

And how very inclusive this turned out to be, for the Bible says, "As he which hath called you is holy, so be ye holy in all manner of conversation" (1 Pet. 1:15). This became even more difficult when I realized that the word "conversation" meant "manner of life." In the American Standard Version it is translated ". . . in all manner of living." In the Weymouth translation it reads ". . . in all your behavior," while the Phillips translation reads ". . . in every department of your lives."

None of these or any other ritualistic or man-made concept of holiness will ever help us achieve holiness. They may help us attain a good level of purity, and may aid us in conforming to the letter of God's Word, but even that apartness from everything that we may classify as unholy will not produce the God-like nature in our lives.

The holiness must come from God himself. Divine holiness is not to be thought of as a mere passive, quiescent state; it is an active impulse, a forthgoing energy. God's holiness becomes the expression of his perfect moral nature and is the basis for his entire self-revelation. If He is going to reveal himself through our holy lives He must impart that active impulse, that forthgoing energy.

But once that has been imparted, it will manifest itself. God's holiness within us will be evidenced in our obedience to his Word. Inward changes will be reflected in our outward character. What God puts in we will work out. Our behavior will reflect our inward holiness.

Section III

COMING INTO HOLINESS

Ye shall therefore be holy.

Leviticus 11:45

CHAPTER NINE

Holiness and Righteous Obedience

In the footnotes of the Polyglot Bible, following Philippians 1:11, which says, "Being filled with the fruits of righteousness. . ." I read, "Everything good in men is the fruit of the Holy Spirit; and where He has his work in their hearts, teaching them to practise piety towards God and righteousness towards men, we may confidently expect that He will carry it forward, *through faith and obedience,* till they are perfect in glory" (emphasis added).

Our obedience brings us to holiness. Peter speaks of the "sanctification of the Spirit *unto* obedience" (1 Pet. 1:2, emphasis added), as though the inner workings of the Spirit actually create a "yes" attitude in our hearts. While God will not violate our free moral agency to force us to do his will, He does commission his Holy Spirit to gently urge, cajole, entice, educate, and warn us. He does not violate our wills, but He often makes us willing to obey, for He knows better than we do that obedience is an early step to holiness.

Among the greatest hindrances to holiness is disobedience to the Word and known will of God. All the processes of sanctification stop during times of rebellion. God does not strike us with a heavenly thunderbolt, He just gently withdraws and lets us do our own thing. Frequently, as the misery of having our own way becomes unbearable, we repent of the sin of disobedience and find his grace to be overwhelming. Usually these areas of stubbornness have to do with outward happiness and success. We have to learn that by the surrender of outward happiness and outward success a man may attain inner success. The spirit of the cross is still the path to the highest righteousness.

Charles Spurgeon preached, "Every work of the Spirit of God upon the new nature aims at the purification, the consecration, the perfecting of those whom God in love has taken to be his own. Yea, more; all the events of Providence around us work towards that one end: for this our joys and our sorrows, for this our pains of body and griefs of heart, for this our losses and our crosses—all these are sacred medicines by which we are cured of the disease of nature, and prepared for the enjoyment of perfect spiritual health. All that befalls us on our road to heaven is meant to fit us for our journey's end. Our way through the wilderness is meant to try us, and to prove us, that our evils may be discovered, repented of, and overcome, and that thus we may be without fault before the throne at last. We are being educated for the skies, meetened for the assembly of the perfect. It doth not yet appear what we shall be; but we are struggling up towards it; and we know that when Jesus shall appear, we shall be like him, for we shall see him as he is. We are rising: by hard wrestling, and long watching, and patient waiting, we are rising into holiness."[22]

When Jesus prayed to the Father, petitioning him to sanctify the believers, He said, "Sanctify them *through thy truth"* (John 17:17, emphasis added). God has joined sanctification and truth together. It has become popular, in some circles, to say that Christianity is a life and not a creed. But Christianity is a life which grows out of truth. Jesus Christ is the way and the truth as well as the life, and He is not properly received unless He is accepted in that threefold character. The Bible, which is God's recorded, written truth, is both a channel for reception of sanctification and a manual for the expression of that holiness. The Scripture alone is absolute truth, essential truth, decisive truth, authoritative truth, undiluted truth, eternal, everlasting truth. Truth given us in the Word of God will sanctify all believers to the end of time: God will use it to that end.

But two factors must accompany this written truth for it to be effectual. First, it must be quickened in our hearts by the Holy Spirit, and second, it must be obeyed in our lives. The laws of God are the directions on the package of life. To disobey means confusion; to obey means fulfillment.

God's command must become our commission, for since God is infinite and eternal, there is no other source of righteousness, justice, law, or holiness. We will either submit to him and go his way or we will have to forever do without his nature, his graces, or his presence.

Because of the extreme finality of disobedience, our loving heavenly Father has provided chastisement to bring us back into conformity with his will. "Furthermore we have had fathers of our flesh which corrected us, and we gave them reverence: shall we not much rather be in subjection unto the Father of spirits, and live? For they verily for a few days chastened us after their own pleasure; but he for our profit, that we might be partakers of his holiness" (Heb. 12:9, 10). Chastened to holiness! If we will not obey of our own free will, and cannot be enticed to obey by the wooings of the Holy Spirit, God the Father will chasten us into obedience to bring us into his holy nature.

Whether we have consented to obey the truth or have been chastened unto obedience Titus says that we must function, ". . . in behaviour as becometh holiness. . ." (Titus 2:3).

In my years of Bible reading I have not found any single chapter that sounds the command to obey unto holiness better than the second chapter of the Book of Titus. In this pastoral epistle Paul urges Titus to exhort the saints to exemplify sanctification of life and holiness of character through obedience to the Word of God. Similar standards of righteousness had already been set for the bishops and deacons in the letters to Timothy, but now Paul urges similar standards upon each church member. Lest there be any misunderstanding as to whom he meant, Paul divided the instructions among the aged men, the aged women, the young women, the young men, and the servants. No one was exempt, for Paul assumed that if they were indeed saints, it should show! "But as for you," Paul wrote, "speak up for the right living that goes along with true Christianity" (Titus 2:1, TLB).

The Aged Men (v. 2)

In stating his plea for demonstrated holiness through obedience to the truth, Paul began with the older men and women of the church. Actually he was merely implementing an earlier observation, "Ye became followers of us, and of the Lord . . . so that ye were ensamples to all that believe. . ." (1 Thess. 1:6, 7). Paul saw the church as a large family where the older children automatically become the example for the younger ones. I know, for I was the oldest in our family and was often told that I had to behave as an example to my brothers and sister. Mother has admitted that many of my spankings spared the younger children the need of a spanking, for they learned by the power of my example. Certainly the mature Christians should set the example for holiness of attitude and righteousness of action for the younger ones of the congregation. What is seen is always far more powerful than what is heard.

Six things are required of these older brethren: be sober; be grave; be temperate; be sound in faith, sound in charity, and sound in patience. *The Living Bible* translates this verse, "Teach the older men to be serious and unruffled; they must be sensible, knowing and believing the truth and doing everything with love and patience." The first three requirements have to do with their demeanor, or bearing, and the final three concern their deportment, or conduct.

A true saint who has matured both in years and in his relationship with God will have a demeanor that is serious, sensible, sober, dignified, and discreet. He should outgrow youthful frivolity without losing his zest for life. He should become serious without losing joy and should have a distinct dignity without pathetic pride. Having tasted of heavenly things should affect his behavior amidst earthly things.

The final three commands are concerned with the deportment of the aged men. Their faith should be unmoveable, their love unhinderable, and their patience inexhaustible. When they move toward God their faith and love should be "soundly established" (Knox translation), and when they move toward man their love and patience should be mature and healthy. They are to be the patriarchs of the faith and patterns to the believer.

The Aged Women (v. 3)

"The aged women likewise . . ." places the same responsibility for manifesting holiness in demeanor and deportment on the matured women as upon the aged men. But their command is developed a little differently. ". . . that they be in behaviour as becometh holiness. . . ," or "in deportment as becometh sacred persons" (The Emphasized New Testament), or "to let their deportment testify to holiness" (Conybeare). Lamsa translates it, "to behave as becomes the worship of God." There can be no doubt that Paul is declaring that the actions of the matured saints should reflect the presence of God in their lives.

I observe that two things are prohibited to these women and two things are required from them. First of all, they were not to be false accusers, or slanderers or scandalmongers, as other translators have put it. *The Living Bible*, simply says, "They must not go around speaking evil of others. . . ." How easy it is to fall into this trap, especially when the responsibilities of the home have lightened with the children gone and with time weighing heavily on their hands. Besides this, the younger generation does things so differently than they were done in grandma's day. But the godly woman will not stoop to gossip, scandal, or critical talk. She should be so full of good news (gospel means "good news") that she won't have time to discuss bad news, much less scandalize her neighbors.

The godly woman (or man) should not be a talebearer. She should get no "kick" out of sharing the failures of other Christians, nor should she enjoy vicarious sinning by discussing the sin of another person. When her mind is clean, her lips will be pure. What a product of holiness!

These older women, if they are to manifest holiness, are also prohibited from heavy drinking. They should know that habit is a species of slavery, and Christ has set us free from slavery. They should not need chemical depressants or stimulants, for they do not wrestle with guilt, nor are they plagued with worry and anxiety. These were nailed to Christ's cross long ago. They have "meat to eat" that the world knows nothing of, so why should they stoop to the world's shabby chemical substitutes? They have learned that holiness is basically a relationship with God, and they know that it was excessive wine that cost Noah the intimate relationship with God.

These aged, godly women are urged to teach "good things." "Teachers of goodness," the *Living Bible* says. "Teachers of that which is good . . . teachers of virtue . . . teachers of what is right . . . of what is noble. . . ," other translators say. This, of course, does not imply that all of them should enter the ministry, but rather, "teaching others by their good ensample," as Knox translates it. The fourth verse especially directs them to be teachers of the young women. How I have watched this work in the churches I have pastored. The simple example of my wife among the women of the congregation began a process of change that probably could not have been effected from the pulpit. They learned much by observing her attitude. It is even more noticeable now that she travels with me throughout the world. Pastors urge me to bring her with me because of the influence she exerts upon the women of the congregation. She would be the first to declare that she is not a teacher, but her life speaks so loudly she really does not need to say anything.

A godly mother is still the best antidote to sin in the home, and worshiping Marys, praying Hannahs, and godly Annas are visual training programs that the church can offer its young people. People who won't read the Bible will read "living epistles." No wonder, then, that the aged women are commanded to "be in behaviour as becometh holiness. . . ."

Young Women (vv. 4, 5)

Next Paul addresses his pleas for demonstrated holiness by righteous living to the young women of the church. First of all, these young women are to be taught to "be sober," which simply means to be sensible or show discretion. *The Living Bible* calls it "to live quietly." I would suppose that it deals with the dissatisfaction and discontent of the young mind with its accompanying ambition and hustle. These young saints need to learn and to manifest that gain is not godliness, "but godliness with contentment is great gain" (see 1 Tim. 6:5, 6). Undue emphasis upon possessions and positions tends to ungodliness. How sad to see that this is the shallow emphasis of so much of today's ministry which purports that our relationship to God will be reflected in our bank account and earthly inventories. After getting a glimpse of heaven, what is there on earth worth striving after?

After these younger women learn something about divine wisdom, they are told to learn how to love their husbands and children. It is futile to assume that all women know how to be loving and affectionate wives and mothers. The Bible knows differently. The Bible says that this is a learned response and then commands it of the women, not because the husband and children are especially worthy of the love, but because manifest love is inseparably linked to divine holiness. She who is holy will be loving. Paul's injunction was merely to direct that love into divinely appointed channels, just as he had done for the men in Ephesians 5. Jesus stated, "By this shall all men know that ye are my disciples, if ye have love one to another" (John 13:35). This is more than shaking hands with the preacher and hugging the church members; it is loving the family unit at home so fervently and purely as to draw attention to the Christ who lives within us. This is not a choice we make; it is a commanded demonstration of holiness.

The following five commands given to the young women are all concerned with their behavior in the environment of the home. "Be discreet . . . be chaste . . . be good . . . be keepers at home . . . and be obedient to their own husbands." When my sister Iverna and I pastored together we used to impress this upon the women, and occasionally we enforced it. If a husband complained to me that his wife was spending so much time at the church (we had daily prayer services) that his house was not being well kept, we used to call the woman out of the prayer meeting and send her home, telling her that godliness was not only in praying and reading the Bible. True holiness will manifest itself in proper management of the home, morals, money, temperament, and spiritual hunger. Holiness is not merely a spiritual feeling; it is a practical life that affects everything we do.

Paul ends his injunctions to the young women by saying that these commands must be obeyed, "that the word of God be not blasphemed" (v. 5). If the testimony given on Sunday is not backed up by the manner of life on Monday it is blasphemous. How seldom do we hear it preached that insubordination in the home is blasphemy in the eyes of God, for it is a refusal to allow the "spirit of holiness" to flow through us in the area of life that is the most important—the home.

Young Men (vv. 6-8)

Having spoken at length to the young women, Paul now turns his attention to the young men. "Be sober minded," Paul says. Weymouth translates that, "In the same way exhort the young men to be self-restrained. . . ," while Moffatt says, "Tell the young men also to be masters of themselves at all points." Paul does not ask the women to be in control and the men to be "at liberty"; he urges a demonstration of holiness that makes self-control a high priority. The young men must be masters of themselves in their sexuality, their ambitions, their frustrations, their spirituality, their finances, etc.

Furthermore, these young men in general, and Titus in particular, are urged to be "a pattern of good works." Having urged the young men "to behave carefully, taking life seriously," *The Living Bible* says, "and here you yourself must be an example to them of good deeds of every kind." Paul did not believe that a man had to be old to manifest a godlikeness. He had instructed young Timothy, "Let no man despise thy youth; but be thou an example of the believers, in word, in conversation, in charity, in spirit, in faith, in purity" (1 Tim. 4:12). I have heard so many young men say that no one will listen to them teach the Word because they are so young. But it isn't age people look for, it is spiritual maturity and ability to teach. If the young person will demonstrate godliness in his life style, with consistency, people will be willing to listen to what is said.

The Living Bible concludes Paul's charge to these young men by saying, "Let everything you do reflect your love of the truth and the fact that you are in dead earnest about it. Your conversation should be so sensible and logical that anyone who wants to argue will be ashamed of himself because there won't be anything to criticize in anything you say!" (vv. 7, 8). Even the way the mind is disciplined is a demonstration of holiness, and the Word commands it. We need to learn to use that "mind of Christ" Paul declares that we have (See 1 Cor. 2:16). Too often we talk of feelings without being able to back it up with facts. True holiness will demonstrate itself more concretely than that.

Servants (vv. 9, 10)

Paul completes his commands to manifest holiness by speaking to the servants in the church. *The Living Bible* puts Paul's practical teaching in these words: "Urge slaves to obey their masters and to try their best to satisfy them. They must not talk back, nor steal, but must show themselves to be entirely trustworthy. In this way they will make people want to believe in our Savior and God" (vv. 9, 10). If this was required of people who were little more than property, and could be bought and sold like beasts, should it not be even more true of employees who are free to work where they like? I used to teach the men of my congregation that it is a demonstration of holiness to be the best worker on the job; to arrive a little early and to be willing to stay a little late if the work load requires it. I urged them to be sparing in their taking of "breaks," and to always be sure that they made the boss more money than they cost him. These men set such a good example that their employers often phoned the church office asking if we had anyone else looking for work. If godliness doesn't work on the job it isn't true godlikeness; it is a religious substitute used only in church.

So this chapter declares that holiness should be demonstrated in our attitudes, deportment, actions, love lives, and in our use of drugs and drink. The way the house is kept, the way the job is worked, and the way we prepare ourselves to "be ready always to give an answer to every man that asketh you a reason of the hope that is in you with meekness and fear" (1 Pet. 3:15) all reveal the depth of our sanctification. Clean morals, contentment with such things as we have, a serious approach to life, and a demonstrated pattern of good works do more to demonstrate holiness than a thousand sermons. The honesty of our speech, the soundness of our faith, especially in times of testing, and the fervency of our love, toward both God and the brethren, are gauges God uses to reveal the effectiveness of our walk with him.

But these things are not commanded of the bishops and the deacons; this chapter is written to the layman. This is not the "super" life that qualifies us for high office; this is the normal life of a sanctified Christian. This is not even the optional life of the "deeper" saint. It is the only life the Bible describes for a saint.

We have already discovered that this life cannot be produced by us; it must be presented to us. Accordingly, Paul goes on to say, in verse 11, "For the grace of God that bringeth salvation hath appeared to all men." It has been imparted, and for those who have responded in faith it has been imputed. The life is a divine life; it is godlikeness; it is holiness. It is not something to be looked forward to but something to be received right here and now. Life has come! That life will change us. It has come to instruct us, to discipline us, to school us, to train us how to live godly. Paul says that this life-grace of God will teach us how to do two things: (1) "deny ungodliness and worldly lusts; and (2) how to live soberly, righteously, and godly, in this present world" (v. 12).

The Two World Systems (vv. 12, 13)

In reviewing commands to holiness, it seems that most of the requirements will conveniently fit into one of these

two categories: denying, or living. Here in Titus 2:12, 13
Paul seems to speak of the two world systems that pull
upon the Christian. In what Paul calls "worldly" or "this
present world" (v. 12) is a trinity that John defines as the
devil, the world, and the flesh (see 1 John 2:14-16). Ruth
Paxson, in her book *Called Unto Holiness*, prefers to
speak of the trinity of the world system thus: "Satan is the
very embodiment of evil and hate. His names and works
show this. He is 'the wicked one,' 'the adversary,' 'the
tempter,' 'a liar,' 'a murderer,' 'a deceiver.' Everything
that he is and does is a manifestation of hate toward Christ
and the Christian. The world partakes of the nature of
Satan. . . .

"But to turn to the other trinity, we find Christ the very
embodiment of holiness and love. All His names and
works show it. . . . Everything that He is and does is the
manifestation of love toward God and toward man.

"The Church partakes of the nature of Christ as He is
living within it now through the power of the Holy Spirit
to make it holy and loving as He is. He will one day
present it unto Himself perfected in holiness and without
blemish" (pp. 18, 19).

It is because of the tremendous contrast between these
two world systems, and the influence they exert upon the
Christian, that Paul exhorts us to learn to deny the first
and embrace the second. If, instead, we embrace the first
we will live a Satan-controlled, world-conformed, and
flesh-centered life. It may be "good" by the standards of
the world, and even very "religious," for Satan is a very
religious being who earnestly desires to be worshiped,
but it cannot be godly because it is not godlike or
God-controlled.

In Paul's command to "deny ungodliness and worldly
lusts," he was reminding us that the flesh (by which he

LET US BE HOLY

meant not the body but the human soul) is both evil and hostile toward God, for Paul had written to the church at Rome, "Because the carnal mind is enmity against God: for it is not subject to the law of God, neither indeed can be. So then they that are in the flesh cannot please God" (Rom. 8:7, 8). As Ruth Paxson says, "Everyone has within him a traitor to God. It is that awful sinful nature, the very essence of which is hostility to God."[23]

Oh, how hard we have tried to please God with our flesh. We have sung, prayed, and preached in dignified, learned flesh, but it could not please God. Whenever we substitute our soulish nature for God's divine Spirit we are doomed to failure, for nothing of this lower order is capable of substituting for the higher, divine order.

Just as Paul told the church at Rome that it is not a controlled mind but a renewed mind that God seeks (see Rom. 12:2), so here he informs the Christians that it is not controlled ungodliness but denied ungodliness, and not controlled lusts but denied lusts, that are required in order to faithfully demonstrate divine holiness. All of the desires, affections, and appetites that govern the men of this world system are to be denied their controlling influence in the lives of men and women who have been made holy. Gluttony, drunkenness, anger, malice, revenge, immoderate love of riches, power, and fame must have no place in our lives. They belong in the world system; we must flee them as we would run from a poisonous serpent. They will never be content to serve us; they are bent upon ruling and ruining us.

The teaching of self-denial is never pleasant nor popular, but it is necessary. We own the controlling voice in our lives. It is we who say "yes," or "no," and the results of that choice affect the entire spectrum of our life and ministry.

Live Righteously in this Present World

Holiness is a positive, not a negative force. It would be possible to get so involved in denial as to become ascetic and still not be holy. God deals with negatives as a doctor deals with disease; his goal is a return to wholeness of life. But, of course, the negatives cannot be ignored; they must be dealt with, both in the natural and in the spiritual. But once the problem has been corrected the future emphasis is on maintaining and manifesting strength of life.

Once we learn to instantly deny ungodliness and worldly lusts (and the force of the Greek is "denying once for all") "we should live soberly, righteously, and godly, in this present world" (v. 12).

We should live *soberly* in respect to ourselves; *righteously* in respect to our neighbor; and *godly* in respect to God. Holiness must manifest itself inwardly, outwardly, and upwardly. It affects my will, my walk, and my worship. It will make me godly in my soul, godly in my social intercourse, and godly in my spiritual responses.

But this is not a loss of life; it is a true living of life. It is a life that is consistently right and righteous in every area and in all manifestations. It is a higher form of life that is lived among creatures animated by a lower form of life, very much as a man lives among his dogs. This can be done in comfort without ever stooping to partake of the dog's nature because of the higher intelligence and abilities of the man. So the Christians can live in this world without having to physically separate themselves from the ungodly, and still maintain their divine life.

Furthermore, the Christian is content to avoid worldly lusts because he is ever "looking for that blessed hope, and the glorious appearing of the great God and our

Saviour Jesus Christ" (v. 13). In the coming world we may gratify every desire without need of self-discipline, because all desire there will be conformable to God's will. There we will really be in our element, surrounded only by those of the same higher nature, and we will be comfortable with God's glorious kingdom.

But we are not yet in that world, we are earth-bound. Or are we? Didn't Jesus tell the Father twice in his high priestly prayer, "They are not of the world, even as I am not of the world"? (John 17:14, 16). Sanctified Christians can be *in* the world but not *of* the world. There is a place in Christ Jesus that lifts us out of the corruption of this world system and lets us enter into the outer periphery of the heavenly life that shall someday be our normal habitat. We are invited, even now, to "Abide in me. . ." (John 15:4).

CHAPTER TEN

Holiness and Abiding

That God is holy is no more satisfying to me than the realization that birds can fly. Birds have long frustrated and at the same time fascinated me, for I cannot remember a time when I didn't long to fly. I still remember in my preschool years when my father was a pastor in Reno, Nevada, that he let church out early one Sunday morning because an aviator was scheduled to fly into the area shortly after noon. We drove to the open field and watched for hours as he took passengers into the air on their first flight. How I begged for a ride, but it was considered far too dangerous for a boy of my age.

I remember the thrill of having a kite in the air tugging on the string in my hand. I used to jump when the tug was especially strong, hoping that the kite might lift me up and carry me for a ride. Something in my spirit always wanted to soar; I was tired of being earthbound.

Like other boys of my day, I jumped off the shed roof, wildly flapping my arms, hoping to be able to fly; and I, too, ruined a perfectly good umbrella trying to sail into the wind on a gusty day. But it was not until I was in the first grade that I got my first chance to really fly. In returning from a visit to my maternal grandparents I spotted a small airfield with a sign advertising rides for daring passengers. I pled so desperately for the chance that dad turned off the road, drove up to the hangar, and stepped inside the small business office to explain to the owner-pilot that his two young boys had a fascination with airplanes, but he was certain they would never actually get in one to fly. The pilot was a father and graciously came out to explain the hazards of flying, and even sat us in the open-front cockpit of the biplane to let us get the "feel" of it. When we refused to get out, dad good-naturedly shelled out the money (two for the price of one) for us to take a ride, having already been promised a refund if we cried to get out before the plane took off.

But there were no cries of terror, only cries of delight, even when the pilot looped the plane, spun it, and dived it. Dad lost his hard-to-come-by depression money, but I gained the first feeling of freedom from the earth's control. I had actually flown in an airplane, and I was never the same again.

Although I was very young, I not only had the thrill of a lifetime, but I learned a very valuable principle: I cannot become a bird, but I can fly if I get into something that is greater than myself that can overcome the pull of gravity.

I have since become a private pilot and have logged flying time in many different models of aircraft, but I am no closer to being able to fly by virtue of my nature or desire than I was in my preschool years. I need to constantly apply the laws of aerodynamics that balance the forces of thrust, lift, drag, and pull to enable me to rise into the sky with more speed, height, and range than most birds. As long as the power is applied, gravity is overridden. In the plane I can fly; out of it I must walk.

Similarly, when I see God's holiness it inspires me to be holy. I feel the tug of the kite string, but it does not lift me from my unholiness. I have tried various jumps from spiritual shed roofs and have flapped my wings "by faith," but I always end up in a heap on the earth again. If ever I attain to God's holiness—and He has commanded me to attain it—I will need to discover a law, or principle, that will release me from the control of my carnal nature.

I believe Paul found this, for he wrote, "For the law of the Spirit of life in Christ Jesus hath made me free from the law of sin and death" (Rom. 8:2). I can well remember the first time that this verse began to speak to my heart. I reacted to it as emotionally as I reacted to my first plane ride. I saw that there was available, in the Spirit of Christ, an overriding force similar to the law of aerodynamics that did not repeal unholiness, any more than aerodynamics repeals the law of gravity, but merely overrode it with a higher power. The more I studied this chapter, the greater became my awareness that God admitted my inability to achieve holiness and so had provided for that holiness through Christ Jesus and the Holy Spirit. I began to see that God, too, had an airplane, which I call "the plane of holiness." There is a process, a force, a principle that can lift me into God's divine nature, but that principle originated in God, not in me.

The key, of course, is learning to abide in Christ. For as surely as the airplane can enable me to rise above the pull of gravity only as long as I remain in it, so Christ can lift me out of the pull of this world system and ungodliness only as I remain firmly fixed in him. There is never any danger of his running out of power to override godliness, as there is the very real fact of life that eventually the airplane will run out of fuel, lose power, and come back under the control of gravity. Ungodliness will never, in this world or the next, gain any control over God. But there is the danger of my stepping out of Christ to attempt to produce my own holiness. That will always produce a fall. It is really "jumping to a conclusion."

Some religious heritages serve "instantism" and crisis experiences as a constant fare, and the hope that is set before us as both the goal to be achieved and the ultimate reward for all Christian discipline is the attainment of heaven. But heaven is never spoken of as the *goal* of Christian living. It is the perfection of Christian character that is so transparently taught by Christ. "Be ye therefore perfect, even as your Father which is in heaven is perfect," He said (Matt. 5:48).

It is sometimes a painfully slow learning process to realize that the work of the Spirit today is to conform, mold, and shape individuals into the likeness and image of God. God is after Christian character—holiness. Paul wrote, "For whom he did foreknow, he also did predestinate to be conformed to the image of his Son" (Rom. 8:29). We are being changed into Christ's image from glory to glory (2 Cor. 3:18), and God will not cease his workings in us "till we all come in the unity of the faith, and of the knowledge of the Son of God, unto a perfect man, unto the measure of the stature of the fulness of Christ" (Eph. 4:13).

We can easily lose sight of the true objective by getting absorbed in the technique, mechanism, and method of trying to attain it. So often our doing is not properly related to God's objective.

John Wright Follette said, "Christian character is never given as a gift. Righteousness is imputed to us on the basis of His redemption, but never Christian character—this is the product of training, overcoming, discipline, trial, hardship, and intensive spiritual living. I cannot work and earn salvation, but I can apply myself to intelligent and spiritual living and build a character. He keeps the goal in mind (even when we fail to do so) and leads us through a thousand experiences to make *in* us a manifestation of His *life*. I cannot earn salvation, but by His grace I can *overcome* and thus become Christ-like in life and character.

"So let us keep this distinction in mind and not deceive ourselves by thinking because we have had certain genuine experiences, such as salvation, the baptism in the Spirit, healing, or consecration, that any one or all can in themselves *give* us character. They are like a series of crises through which the Holy Spirit leads the hungry heart in its quest for truth. These experiences are open doors through which we pass (no one is finality). We must surrender to the *purpose* of the crisis—yield to the Holy Spirit and be *taught* and walk in the Spirit and possess our inheritance."[24]

When David cried, "Lord, who shall abide in thy tabernacle?" (Ps. 15:1), the answer was that it was the man whose walk, works, words, will, and handling of his wealth had been brought into harmony with God's word.[25] It takes an adjustment in life style (not culture) to remain in the presence of the Lord. But remaining in that divine presence is the key to holiness. *Where* we are determines *what* we are. Ruth Paxson says, "One thing, and only one thing, determines where you are. It is your relation to the crucified, risen, ascended, exalted Savior and Lord."[26]

The one thing that matters most is whether a man will really accept the God who will make him holy. At all costs a man must be rightly related to God. The more we pray, "Lord, show me what holiness means for me," the more He will show us that it means being made one with Jesus. Holiness is not something Jesus Christ puts into me; it is *himself* in me. As Oswald Chambers puts it, "Sanctification does not mean anything less than the holiness of Jesus being made mine manifestly. The one marvellous secret of a holy life lies not in imitating Jesus, but in letting the perfections of Jesus manifest themselves in my mortal flesh. Sanctification is 'Christ in you.' "27

In the teaching of Christ on the vine and the branch (in John 15), Christ defines himself as the true vine and describes his Father as the caretaker or farmer. He calls us the branch upon which the fruit is to be displayed. The fruit will bear the characteristics of the central stock, for all of the life source flows through the "true vine." The nature of the vine is transmitted through the branch by virtue of a process of "abiding," or remaining connected. The farmer will prune, cleanse, disinfect, and tie up the branch, but he will never sever it, for he knows that would end all fruitfulness.

Our main responsibility in being holy is to remain vitally and intimately connected to the Lord Jesus Christ. When we are in intimate union with him, His nature will flow through us naturally. It is not a struggle to bear the divine fruit of holiness; it is the natural outgrowth of an intimate relationship with God. Jesus said it so simply: "I am the vine, ye are the branches: He that abideth in me, and I in him, the same bringeth forth much fruit: for without me ye can do nothing" (John 15:5).

We need not pray to find if this is the will of God for our life, for the Word declares, "This is the will of God, even your sanctification" (1 Thess. 4:3). It is never a question of whether God is willing to sanctify us; the question is always, is it *my* will? Am I willing to let God do in me all that has been made possible through Christ's becoming "a root out of a dry ground" (Isa. 53:2)? Am I willing to bear the fruit of holiness and submit to the hand of the vinedresser for whatever pruning he deems necessary for the production of the best quality fruit? Our answers to these questions will determine the level of our attainment of God's holiness.

Sanctification makes us one with Jesus Christ, and in him one with God, and it produces glorious effects of obedience, service, prayer, and speechless adoration, but we must guard against the temptation of putting the effect as the cause. The cause is a new relationship; the effect is a new response. Our response did not produce the relationship; it was the relationship that produced the response.

A godly man of a past generation, who is unknown to me, wrote some comments about Paul's statement, "Godliness is profitable unto all things" (1 Tim. 4:8). The well-worn note that I have carried for a long time reads, "This is the goal to which all exercise in godliness must tend—godly habits, a godlike character, *and a fitness for the work which God has for us to do.* It was for this that Jesus Christ lived and died. It was to redeem us from all iniquity, to bring us to God, to conform us to his own likeness. We must live much in the life of Jesus Christ; we must meditate more often on his character and work. . . . For the best efforts, the most noble self-denial will be in vain unless we are in touch with Jesus Christ as the sole source of power" (emphasis mine).

Certainly one of the goals toward which godliness must reach is effective Christian witness. It has been charged, with some validity, that those who strive for perfection in the Christian life seem to lack any drive for evangelism. It is suggested that they have become so introspective that they have lost sight of the "go" in the gospel. But true Christian witness can hardly be avoided by one who has come into a measure of God's holiness. Jesus told his disciples, "But ye shall receive power, after that the Holy Ghost is come upon you: *and ye shall be* witnesses unto me both in Jerusalem, and in all Judaea, and in Samaria, and unto the uttermost part of the earth" (Acts 1:8, emphasis added). He did not so much say they would *do witnessing* as He declared that they would *be witnesses*. Christian witness starts with being something outstanding, different, other-worldly. Holiness produces all of that.

CHAPTER ELEVEN

Holiness and Christian Witness

Because of my religious heritage my concepts of the Holy Spirit were formed early in my life. I cannot remember a time when the gifts and graces of the Spirit were not taught and demonstrated during my boyhood days. My father, who was the only pastor I ever had until I entered the ministry, regularly preached on the Spirit, and what are now viewed as the charismatic phenomena were common practices in his churches.

As I remember it, great emphasis used to be placed on the *Holy* Spirit. I do not remember testimonies to "being filled with the Spirit," as are common today; it was always "the Holy Spirit." He was viewed as God, and God is intrinsically holy; holiness is characteristic of God's moral nature. It is to be anticipated, then, that all of his attitudes, actions, and abilities would be exercised in holiness and toward the production and expression of holiness in the lives of Christians. This seems to be the story of New Testament Christianity, and it fits my memory of the lives of the early Pentecostals.

LET US BE HOLY

Whenever the Holy Spirit was given entrance to the lives of these early believers there were consistent changes in their behavior patterns. Sometimes the changes were quite radical and dramatic. I can remember that some merchants in the town would rejoice when a "Holy Ghost revival" would hit the community, for it meant that many back bills and old debts would be paid up, and that people who had stolen merchandise over the years would make restitution for it after the Holy Spirit came into their lives. Other merchants, however, dreaded the coming of such a revival, for it often forced the closing of saloons, theaters, dance halls, and other places of worldly amusements since no one would attend. Under the impetus of the Spirit's inner workings, sins were confessed, marriages were straightened out, dishonesty ceased, and workmen gave their employers a full day's labor, and then some. Newspaper advertisements were not needed to awaken the community to the special services since the changed lives of the residents of the community were a far more powerful witness than any advertising.

Because my father was a Spirit-filled holiness preacher who often took me to conventions with him, I have had the privilege of sitting repeatedly under the ministry of such men and women of God as Smith Wigglesworth, Aimee Semple McPherson, Dr. Charles Price, and many others. They were powerful preachers of the Word of God. They didn't do much entertaining; I don't remember their expertise at telling jokes or stories, but I can remember squirming uncomfortably as they preached against sin under the anointing of the Holy Spirit. I can remember their positive assertion that the Holy Spirit came into our lives to represent a holy God and that this demanded a holy life. I can remember mass altar calls where people went forward to be renewed in the "Spirit of holiness" (Rom. 1:4) and can recall all-night prayer meetings as people sought to be made more godlike in both their inner and outer natures.

Through the years that have followed I have seen a decline in the emphasis upon holiness. "Were these 'old-time' preachers extremists?" I have asked myself a thousand times. "Were they striving for the unattainable? Were they demanding a level of righteousness that can be achieved only in the heavens? Were their standards too high?"

But I can't argue with their results. They cleaned up entire towns without becoming social activists. They closed dens of iniquity without resorting to court action. They resolved adulterous habits without divorce, and enforced restitution without coercion or threats. They did not emphasize the prayer language as much as the private life. They accepted emotional responses, which were many, varied, and often glorious, but they expected transformed lives as well. A familiar statement during those days of revival was, "I don't care how high you jump as long as you walk a straight line when you come down." Shouting that was not the outgrowth of a holy life was considered a work of the flesh and was often ruled out of order in the service. They felt that godly lives were a prerequisite to godly responses.

Were they really extremists in their demands for holiness? Today's generation would probably think so, but I can attest that many of them were examples of what they preached. My father used to have some of these godly men and women in our home, and I had the chance to observe them from the nonthreatening position of a small boy. I watched the way they treated their wives and my mother. I listened to them talk around the table when they were safely away from their public; I marveled at their stories and laughed at their jokes. But I must admit that my memory cannot recall any unholiness among them. Oh, there were fakes, of course. There always will be. But the rewards for a ministry in holiness were not commercially attractive enough to attract many charlatans. For the most part, those who preached holiness practiced it scrupulously, and they not only lived it, they liked it. Holiness did not separate them from happiness; it seemed to be the basic source of their inner joy.

Were they really extreme, or were they merely following the pattern given by the early church in the Book of Acts? Peter's sermon on the day of Pentecost didn't tell anyone how to get wealthy, remain healthy, or have a more enjoyable sex life, but it did produce a great conviction of sin. Acts 2:37 reads, "Now when they heard this, they were pricked in their heart, and said unto Peter and to the rest of the apostles, Men and brethren, what shall we do?" Peter's answer was for them to repent, be baptized, and receive the Holy Ghost (Acts 2:38). There is no question in my mind that the church had its beginning in holiness, for sin was dealt with ("repent"), lives were expected to change ("be baptized"), and divine assistance was called upon to achieve these goals ("and receive the Holy Ghost").

This emphasis upon pure lives and righteous living was no deterrent to the life of the church, for Dr. Luke tells us that about three thousand converts were added to the church that day and that fear and awe overwhelmed the residents of Jerusalem (Acts 2:41, 43). Whenever we read of these early apostles being plagued, persecuted, or pressured, we also read of another special coming of the Holy Spirit to redirect, release, or reassure them. Also, none was allowed to function in deceit or hypocrisy, as Ananias and Sapphira sadly learned (Acts 5:1-11), for the presence of the Holy Spirit rapidly unmasked all falsehood.

During the years that I have traveled alternately among the classic-Pentecostals and the neo-Pentecostals, I have often been asked by some of the older members of the Pentecostal community if I sincerely believe that the Spirit that is being received today is the same Spirit that was poured out some sixty or so years ago. They, too, are concerned at the apparent lack of holiness in the lives of those who are being filled with the Holy Spirit in this generation. My answer to them is the obvious one, for there is only one Spirit of God, and anyone who is genuinely filled with the Spirit according to the Bible pattern has received the same Spirit of holiness that moved entire communities godward in past generations. The change is not in the Holy Spirit, for Malachi 3:6 declares, "I am the Lord, I change not. . . ." He is as much the Spirit of holiness today as He was when He anointed Jesus, indwelt Peter, inspired Paul, or infused John on the isle of Patmos.

No, it is not the Spirit that is different; it is man's surrender to that Spirit. Perhaps we are more interested in his power and his gifts (what we can get from him) than we are in his basic nature. Maybe we have not been taught sufficiently that his divine ministry should be not only through us for others but to us for ourselves. I wonder if today's church may have overlooked the truth that we have been called "according to his purpose," which is "to be conformed to the image of his Son . . ." (Rom. 8:28, 29). The Holy Spirit has come to do not our will, but the will of the Father, and that will is that we be made in the divine image so that the fellowship which was destroyed by sin can be restored through righteousness.

How often have I heard the old holiness preachers declare that the fundamental purpose of the coming of the Holy Spirit, to the world in general and the Church in particular, is to restore man to the presence of God, and step one is to restore him to the image and likeness of God. I can readily concur with them. The main product of the Holy Spirit is holiness; a glorious by-product is evangelism. His main purpose is to develop God's image in the saints; his pleasure is to distribute God's gifts to these saints to enable them to quickly come into that image. Oftentimes he seems to lavishly display the by-products in order to motivate man into a receptivity of the main product, but if holiness is summarily refused the giftings are surely revoked. Such, at least, seems to be the history of revivals from the days of Martin Luther to the present. Evangelism, enthusiasm, and enablements are directly tied to holiness. "You can't have one without the other." When our lives no longer reflect the holiness of God, they will no longer receive the blessings of God. Only through an increased production of the main product can we achieve an increase of the by-products. Evangelism will automatically increase outside the church when holiness increases inside her.

In the Book of Acts the disciples were not engaged in "evangelism" as we tend to use the word. They hired no stadiums, conducted no crusades, offered no religious concerts, and didn't even have a "committee for evangelism." And yet they won converts to the Lord Jesus Christ by the thousands. The rulers of the Jews "took knowledge of them, that they had been with Jesus" (Acts 4:13). There was something of the divine nature that radiated through these common men. It was the supernatural life within them that was attractive, not their doctrine or practices. Some of these early Christians won more converts to Christ through their martyrdom than some groups have won through their missionary endeavors.

I do not mean to downgrade modern methods of evangelism. I am only pointing out that long before such refined methods were known evangelism was effective. But the effectiveness of the early ministry was in the display of Christ Jesus in the life of the messenger, and so it must be today. Methods do not win people to Christ, holy, anointed men win others to Jesus. All methods must remain secondary to the main force of our Christian witness—manifesting something of Christ to those who see and hear.

In speaking to wives, Peter said, "Wives, fit in with your husbands' plans; for then if they refuse to listen when you talk to them about the Lord, they will be won by your respectful, pure behavior. Your godly lives will speak to them better than any words" (1 Pet. 3:1, TLB). A wife does not need a Bible school certificate to be able to win her husband to Christ, she merely needs a holy life that manifests Christ on a day-to-day basis.

Our godly behavior does not excuse us from doing personal witnessing; it opens the door for it. Instead of trying to "convince" everyone we meet, our life can be used of the Holy Spirit to begin a work of conviction, and then that person will be receptive to what we tell them about Jesus and God's plan of salvation. Until we live it there is not much value in lipping it, for our behavior out-shouts our sales pitch.

Worldly businesses have long known that the best advertising they can get is a satisfied customer. Jesus Christ knew this long before businessmen picked it up. He would have the husbandman first become a partaker of the fruits (2 Tim. 2:6). When we are partakers of the divine nature we demonstrate it, we declare it, we testify to it; we enjoy it. We are like the young couple with their first baby, we must show it off to everyone.

We know that holiness and love are inseparable. Both are manifestations of the divine nature, and both are offered to the Christian and are expected to be revealed in his life. Jesus declared that it would be this revelation of the indwelling nature of God that would convince men of the world that we were indeed disciples of Christ. In John 13:35 he said, "By this shall all men know that ye are my disciples, if ye have love one to another." Would not this suggest that expressing and sharing the holy nature of God with the brotherhood of believers is, in itself, a powerful Christian witness?

CHAPTER TWELVE

Holiness Is Achievable

After Paul told the church at Philippi about his deep yearnings to win Christ and be found in him, and to actually know him, he said, "Brethren, I count not myself to have apprehended: but this one thing I do, forgetting those things which are behind, and reaching forth unto those things which are before, I press toward the mark for the prize of the high calling of God in Christ Jesus. Let us therefore, as many as be perfect [mature], be thus minded. . . . (Phil. 3:13-15).

Paul did not consider himself to have arrived, to have achieved the ultimate. He continued to press, to climb, to rise higher into the nature of God. Furthermore, he invites us to do so, too.

But if there is more to be received; if there are greater realms of divine holiness to be imparted; if there are higher levels of God's righteousness to be displayed, then there must be means offered by which we can achieve them.

LET US BE HOLY

The Blood of Christ Brings Us to Holiness

A glorious part of the process of bringing us into that holy nature is the "sprinkling of the blood of Jesus Christ." That our sanctification is based fully upon the justification purchased by the death of Christ Jesus has been clearly established in chapter four. The deliverance of men from a state of sin and death by making them alive to holiness is of God. It springs from his love, was purchased through the death of his Son, is the fruit of his Spirit, and is given not merely to save men from hell, but to manifest in all ages and throughout the world the riches of his grace, in kindness to believers, through Jesus Christ. Holiness in man apart from the work of Christ's cross is unthinkable.

In his second epistle, Peter wrote, "According as his divine power hath given unto us all things that pertain unto life and godliness through the knowledge of him that hath called us to glory and virtue" (1:3). It is not through the mere ritual of sprinkling of blood, but through the knowing of the Christ of the blood of sprinkling, that we have received all things that pertain unto godliness. The death of Christ is only one part of his passion that released men from sin and restored them to fellowship with God. He who died rose again, and now "he ever liveth to make intercession for them" (Heb. 7:25). I have had repeated occasions to learn that the blood of Jesus Christ is a powerful force to bring us to holiness, for it is God's answer to sin, it is one of our weapons against Satan, and becomes the symbol on the doorposts of our hearts that we are among the covenant people who are to be spared the judgment of God. No wonder we used to sing with such emotion, "Thank God for the blood, that washes white as snow."

Faith Brings Us to Holiness

In his writings, Peter many times refers to faith as being an active agent in bringing us to holiness. Here in this first chapter of his first epistle he speaks of the "trial of your faith . . . [being] found unto praise and honour and glory . . ." (v. 7); of "receiving the end of your faith, even the salvation of your souls" (v. 9); and "that your faith and hope might be in God" (v. 21). For several months, while God was dealing in this realm of faith for holiness, I preached from 2 Peter 1 where the statement "whereby are given unto us exceeding great and precious promises: that by these ye might be partakers of the divine nature" (v. 4) is followed with the challenge to "add to your faith virtue . . . knowledge . . . temperance . . . patience . . . godliness . . . brotherly kindness . . . charity. For if these things be in you, and abound, they make you that ye shall neither be barren nor unfruitful in the knowledge of our Lord Jesus Christ" (vv. 5-8).

It became unmistakably plain to me that a clear operation of faith was essential if I was to be a partaker of God's holy nature. My fears had to give way to faith. Romans 1:17 declares, "For therein is the righteousness of God revealed from faith to faith: as it is written, The just shall live by faith," while Romans 3:22 says, "Even the righteousness of God which is by faith of Jesus Christ unto all and upon all them that believe. . . ."

If God's righteousness is revealed from one level of faith to another and can come to man only through the appropriation of faith, and if righteousness is the nature of God expressed to and through mankind, then it becomes imperative that my faith levels rise.

I suppose that one of my personal problems was my past training to have faith in God for *things*. I had faith for healing, faith for finances, faith for anointings, and so forth, but now I had to learn to simply have faith in the very nature of God himself. This, of course, required a restudy of the doctrine of God. I had God in a box, but He didn't fit. At first it was very unsettling to my sense of security to allow some of my prior concepts of God to slip away, but as they were replaced with more accurate concepts, I was strengthened. I found that I needed to know the object of my faith before my faith could become very potent. If what I yearned for was his nature, then I needed to know something about that nature, for, as Jesus said, "According to your faith be it unto you" (Matt. 9:29).

As God began to move me from faith to faith, I discovered that faith is great because it allies man with God. Faith is union with Christ, and this union involves and guarantees increasing Christ-likeness, and Christ-likeness is righteousness. I also had to learn that the righteousness of God, which is to be man's righteousness, does not come by imitation, nor does it come because of a "love that will not let me go," for the candle that stays burning in the window gives no assurance that the prodigal will ever come home.

What is needed is the gift of faith (and the New Testament surely says that even faith is a gift) that will enable a man to respond to the example and answer to the love. But what is faith?

Faith means that one accepts Christ, and this in turn means that he accepts the fact that what He has done for mankind needed to be done. It is not merely repeating statements of faith, for that never changed lives very much. But when true faith operates, three things happen in our lives: (1) We accept God's view as our own on the true nature of our need; (2) we accept his solution to the problem; (3) we accept the fact (and this is where pride, the deadliest of the sins, is broken) that there is no hope at

all in any of our own righteousness which we might wish to
bring forward—and so we rest, or trust entirely, on the
finished work of Christ. There is nothing to negotiate,
nothing to offer to the whole transaction, except our sin,
and certainly we do not argue our worthiness.

In the final analysis a Christian is one who accepts
Christ as the Word (*logos*) on all things. We must learn to
reason, "This is what had to be done; this is what was
done; where do I will to stand in relationship to it?" This
kind of faith sanctifies, for Acts 26:18 speaks of those
"which are sanctified by faith. . . ."

In realizing that by faith, sanctification becomes a
process whereby Christ's pure humanity increasingly
becomes a part of ours, we accept that the righteousness
of sanctification is basically a relationship, never an
attainment. The condition of any man is always the same:
one of total dependence. Faith really means that men
have no security except as they hold on, or better, are
held on to. As John Oman expresses it, "It is not so much a
question of the rung of the ladder which we occupy, but
whether we are climbing or falling." Christian
righteousness is never an attainment; it is a direction, a
loyalty, a commitment, a hope—and someday an arrival.
But faith in God produces faith in the process, and we are
content as long as we are ascending from faith to faith.

It is by faith that the "exceeding great and precious
promises" are appropriated into our lives. It is not what
we read, but what we can respond to and make real in our
lives. Romans 10:17 says, "So then faith cometh by
hearing, and hearing by the word of God." The Greek
word used here for "word of God" is *rhema*, which means
"a saying, a speech." It refers to the word going forth or
being spoken. Faith does not come by merely reading, but
by "hearing." It is not until the Spirit speaks it into my

heart anew that faith begins to flow.

How often, when we are in prayer, the Spirit speaks portion of the Scriptures to us, and it is as though we had never heard it before. It was new, fresh, exciting, and very living. Although we may have read it many hundreds of times, it had never been "spoken" to our hearts, so it had never produced faith.

It is very important to couple prayer with our Bible reading, for unless there comes a quickening and a making alive of the pages of the book, we will merely inform our intellect, not inspire our faith. But when the Spirit and the Word agree; when the book becomes a talking book; when the Scriptures read like a love letter from home, then faith streams like rays of light from the sun. We seldom find it hard to believe God for anything He has said to us. That very speaking produces faith in our hearts. God totally believes in everything that He says, and that faith flows with his words. All that we need to do after hearing from God's quickened Word is to say what He said, to confess and express that faith in believing participation and in active appropriation of what He has promised us.

In commenting on Paul's statement, "But of him are ye in Christ Jesus, who was made unto us wisdom from God, and righteousness, and sanctification, and redemption" (1 Cor. 1:30, RV), W.E. Evans wrote, "Christ is indeed all these things to us, but in reality, He becomes such only as we appropriate Him for ourselves. Only as the believer, daily, yea, even momentarily, takes by faith the holiness of Jesus, His faith, His patience, His love, His grace, to be his own for the need of that very moment, can Christ who by His death was made unto him sanctification in the instantaneous sense, become unto him sanctification in the progressive sense—producing in the believer His own life moment by moment. Herein lies the secret of a holy life—the momentary appropriation of Jesus Christ in all the riches of His grace for every need as it arises. The degree of our sanctification is the proportion of our appropriation of Christ."[28]

To this we can only join in the cry of the disciples to Jesus: "Lord, increase our faith" (Luke 17:5).

From the James Hastings four-volume *Dictionary of the Bible*, copyrighted in 1901, I copied this paragraph and carried it with me for many months: "Man is urged to work out the grace within; yet with an awful sense that God Himself is already at work, prompting and animating, and so in utter reliance on His mighty initiative. A moral conflict there is, a struggle that taxes the nerves of the soul and exercises all its vigilance; but it is a conflict *of faith* (1 Tim. 6:12), conducted in reliance upon Divine resources (Christ, and the Holy Spirit ever taking of His things and inspiring the soul), not in self-sufficiency (see Gal. 2:20 in contrast to Rom. 10:2; 7:7; 8:9; 3:27). The normal, and not only the intermittent, issue of such a conflict may be victory, and that without prescribed limit. Failure is due to imperfection of receptivity, intermittent 'abiding.' Yet, where this is understood, failure but strengthens for fuller victory, by deepening the sense of dependence; 'for when I am weak, then am I strong' (2 Cor. 12:10)."

However great the struggle of faith, we can learn to be comfortable that He who is the beginner of faith is also the finisher of that faith (Heb. 12:2). There is, of course, a sense in which the believer is responsible for his progress in the Christian life; yet it is also true that, after all, it is the divine grace which works it all in him. We cannot purify ourselves, but we can yield to God and then the purity will come. At times it seems that I can hear Paul saying, "God, by his mighty power, will do for you what I, by my admonitions, and you, by your own efforts, cannot do." So if we major in staying close enough to Christ to hear what He says, we know that faith will flow with his communication, and that faith will be a powerful agent in our sanctification.

Love Brings Us to Holiness

How many times I have been asked, "How can I get my faith to work?" My answer is always Galatians 5:6, "faith which worketh by love." Faith and love are repeatedly connected in the New Testament, for love *for* God will become a channel for faith to flow into man, while the love *of* God becomes a channel for that faith to flow into the needy areas of life.

When I was ambitiously aspiring to higher and higher levels of faith, God began to speak to me about love. Every message He gave me for the congregation was on love. When I asked him why He no longer spoke to me of faith, He told me that He would not allow me to become overbalanced on either faith or love. They are like the oars of a boat, or the wings of a bird. They must pull together or you will get nowhere for your efforts.

Love is as much a part of the essential nature of God as holiness is. Some theologians harmonize the two, while others sharply contrast them—holiness being regarded as the self-preservative or retributive attribute of God, and love as his beneficent, self-imparting attribute. But in our limited understanding of the nature of God it seems that these are but two words which best express God's moral perfection, and the difference between them seems more formal than real. In the New Testament, righteousness seems to be an activity or an aspect of love. Righteousness is an element of love without which love would be mere benevolence or good nature. There is a watering down of the true Bible concept of the love of God in much of today's ministry. Divine love is eternally holy and is a consuming fire to all sin. Anything that belittles or obliterates the holiness of God by a false view of the love of God is untrue to the revelation of God given by Jesus Christ.

For instance, we have to guard against the projected idea that Jesus Christ stands with us against God out of pity and compassion, or that He became a curse for us out of sympathy for us. The truth is that Jesus Christ became a curse for us by the divine decree of the Father. Jesus Christ hates the wrong in man, and Calvary is the estimate of his hatred. Conversely, God the Father and Jesus Christ the Son love men. God is for man, but not as a sinner—only as a potential saint. His love for the man did not diminish his hatred for the sin, and Calvary was his method of separating the sin from the sinner so He could condemn the sin while sanctifying the sinner. "But God commendeth his love toward us, in that, while we were yet sinners, Christ died for us" (Rom. 5:8).

It seems, then, that sanctification which begins subjectively as faith, or trustful self-abandonment to God's revealed will, ends as love. Attitude passes to character, the soul becoming assimilated to its object, the God to whom it is consecrated. We believed in him, and now have received love from him. It is the first fruit of the Spirit to ripen in the life of the believer (Gal. 5:22), and it is the characteristic nature of God that convinces the outside world that we are truly Christian, for Jesus said, "By this shall all men know that ye are my disciples, if ye have love one to another" (John 13:35). Likely it is the most enjoyed facet of the nature of God, for it lightens all the dark places of life, restores joy where only despondency reigned, and becomes a channel of expression where there was none before. It is illumination to the spirit, excitement to the soul, and strength to the body, and therefore it becomes health to the entire man. Life without it is not worth living.

But there are definite responsibilities that come with love. One is separateness unto God, for God is a jealous God (Exod. 20:5). I used to see this as small-mindedness far beneath the majesty of almighty God. But as I matured I came to realize that jealousy goes hand in hand with love and need not be small-minded. One who really loves, for that very love's sake, simply cannot suffer the presence of anyone or anything that will harm or destroy or even so much as mar the beloved.

When God said, "Thou shalt have no other gods before me" ("in my presence"—Exod. 20:3), it was not because the almighty God was afraid of the competition. He feared what any perfect lover would fear—that anything less than God would become a destroyer. The danger of false gods is a false life. The Bible clearly commands us to "love not the world, neither the things that are in the world. If any man love the world, the love of the Father is not in him" (1 John 2:15). Furthermore, it tells us that "thou shalt love the Lord thy God with all thy heart, and with all thy soul, and with all thy mind, and with all thy strength: this is the first commandment." This doesn't leave much room for loving something less than God.

All four Gospel writers record the incident when Mary of Bethany anointed the head and feet of Jesus. The love she showered on him with her sacrificial gift, her tears of adoration, and her tenderness are beautiful examples of true worship. But Luke records Jesus as saying, "Her sins, which are many, are forgiven; for she loved much." It was the flow of her love that became the channel for her forgiveness.

A second responsibility that is remanded upon us when

we accept the divine quality of love is that we are expected to be obedient. Jesus said, "If ye love me, keep my commandments" (John 14:15), and "If a man love me, he will keep my words" (John 14:23). It is not "sloppy agape" but "obeying agape" that God wants flowing in our lives.

When we began to realize that love will force us to withdraw from everything that is inconsistent with the nature of God and will become the motivating force for obeying his every request, we will begin to realize what a powerful agent to sanctification love actually is.

Truth Brings Us to Holiness

When Paul wrote about "speaking the truth in love, [we] may grow up into him in all things . . ." (Eph. 4:15), he connected love and truth as companion agents in our maturing into the image of Christ Jesus. Peter declares that we are "born again . . . by the word of God, which liveth and abideth for ever" (1 Pet. 1:23), and Jesus prayed to the Father, "Sanctify them through thy truth: thy word is truth" (John 17:17).

Our sanctification is limited by our restricted knowledge of the Word and by our lack of obedience to God's Word. The most accessible agent of our sanctification, at least to this generation of English-speaking people, is God's Word, and yet it is sadly neglected. Just how does the Word of God sanctify? By revealing sin; by awakening conscience; by revealing the character of Christ; by showing the example of Christ; by offering the influences and powers of the Holy Spirit; and by setting forth spiritual motives and ideals. There is no power like that of the Word of God for detaching a man from the world, the flesh, and the devil.

A notation in the margin of a very old Polyglot Bible

LET US BE HOLY

says, "As divine truth is the great means of sanctification, the more clearly it is understood and the more faithfully it is obeyed, the more holy men will be, the more lovely will be their character, and the greater their usefulness and enjoyment."

I can certainly attest to that. Over and over again God has brought me to his book to instruct me in the conduct of my life. I have found instruction for my financial life, my recreational life, my sexuality, my home life, my ministry, my prayer life, and so forth. I have also been brought face to face with specific commandments in God's Word that could not be disobeyed without a loss of some measure of holiness. I have also found great cleansing in God's Word. When I fail, I find forgiveness in the Word. When I am weak, I find strength; when I am discouraged, I find comfort; and when I am simply defiled by life, I find that Christ still "sanctifies and cleanses it [me] with the washing of water by the word" (Eph. 5:26). Just as He said to his disciples, I have heard Jesus say, "Now ye are clean through the word which I have spoken unto you" (John 15:3).

An anonymous author of the 1800s commented, "Men are said to be sanctified by faith, sanctified through the truth. This cannot be understood so long as we conceive of the human soul as a material substance that becomes brighter, more fruitful, or more fragrant, according to some supposed mysterious action of the Holy Spirit upon it. But if we look at the soul as brought to understand and believe the truth about Christ, his person, his cross, and his work, then we see how soon it becomes like Christ; for it is only by the truth acting upon it that a rational soul can become enlightened, affectionate, devout, as Christ was. A soul that understands and believes the truth must become like him, 'holy, harmless, undefiled, and separate

142

from sinners.' The Spirit does not sanctify us by putting some mysterious principle into our hearts called grace. The *truth* is the grace that he puts into our hearts, and out of this comes every other which deserves the name, even all the features of Christ's image—'love, joy, peace, longsuffering, gentleness, goodness, faith, meekness, temperance.' "

When I meditate on such writings as this, I join David in singing, "Lead me in thy truth, and teach me: for thou art the God of my salvation; on thee do I wait all the day" (Ps. 25:5).

Beholding Christ Brings Us to Holiness

Peter's seventh means of grace that brings us to holiness is given in verse 8: "Whom having not seen, ye love; in whom, though now ye see him not, yet believing, ye rejoice with joy unspeakable and full of glory." It is the upward look, however cloudy or distorted, that effects radical changes in the inner nature.

The unknown writer of the past century whom I quoted above continued to say, "The Apostle Paul [gives us] perhaps the most beautiful description of sanctification in the whole Bible," and then he refers us to 2 Corinthians 3:18: "But we all, with open face beholding as in a glass the glory of the Lord, are changed into the same image from glory to glory, even as by the Spirit of the Lord."

Simply beholding in the mirror of the Word "with open face," in total honesty, with nothing restricting our view, transforms us into what we behold. This is consistent with John's testimony, for he said, "Beloved, now are we the sons of God, and it doth not yet appear what we shall be: but we know that, when he shall appear, we shall be like him; for we shall see him as he is" (1 John 3:2). Beholding, we are changed. When we see him, we shall be like him.

LET US BE HOLY

I had long known that given a certain natural disposition, and given exceptionally favorable circumstances, men may become saintly, but Paul declares that "we *all*" can be changed into the image of the Lord. However, this change does not come through striving but through seeing. It is while we behold Christ in his Word that we are changed, but it is possible to faithfully read the Word without seeing Jesus at all.

Many years ago I took a course in Bible prophecy in Southern California Bible College, where Sister Mildred Ginn spent months opening the Book of Revelation to the class. Although she was known for giving comprehensive examinations, our final examination consisted of but one solitary question: "Show, chapter by chapter, how the Book of Revelation unveils Jesus to our eyes." The complaints from the class almost turned into a protest demonstration. We were prepared to discuss the beast, the false prophet, the Antichrist, and so forth, but most of the class had failed to see Jesus in it even though it is "the revelation of Jesus Christ."

It is easy to see psalms, prophecies, portions of history, promises, patterns for living, and philosophy for Christians without ever seeing Jesus in the mirror of God's Word. But we are changed into God's likeness only by beholding God. "We are changed into the same image. . . ." What we behold, we become.

This was greatly reinforced in me some years ago during a protracted ministry of many months in Australia. I became quite ill—probably a combination of tension and my natural sensitivity to eucalyptus, which abounds on that continent. One morning the Lord instructed me to spend the day in his Word. When I asked if there was any special portion I should read, He directed me to the Book of Colossians. I got dressed, set up a card table, and began to read the book through. When I finished, the Lord asked me what I had seen. My answer did not satisfy him, so I read it through again, this time taking copious notes. But again my answers didn't satisfy him. I borrowed a few modern speech translations from the pastor in whose home I was staying and read the book through in all of them. Still my expanding notebook did not contain the answer God was searching for.

In desperation I cried, "What do you want me to see in Colossians, Lord?"

"I want you to see me," He answered.

"Then open my eyes, please, and cause me to behold you."

As I began to reread this short book I saw Jesus in nearly every verse. Out of that revelation came a series of fifteen messages on Jesus from the first chapter alone, and an additional thirty on the rest of the book. I am now in the process of writing a book on this revelation.

I became so enthusiastic with this unveiling of Christ to my eyes that I spent the rest of the day at that table writing notes as fast as my pen would race across the paper. When it was time for the evening service, I discovered that I was healed. All of the swelling had gone down, I could breathe without difficulty, the rash that had covered great portions of my body had disappeared, and my energy level had risen. While beholding Christ in the Word I was changed—even physically.

The context that precedes this poignant portraiture of sanctification tells the story of Moses coming down from the mount, where he had been speaking with God, his face ablaze with the glory of God (Exod. 34:29-35). It seems that the very pores of his skin had absorbed the radiant energy of God's glory and reflected it to the elders of Israel very much as a mirror catches the rays of the sun and reflects it into the eyes of an onlooker. To the elders, who had never been in the realized presence of God, it was too much, for looking at the face of Moses was like looking straight into the face of God, so Moses put a veil over his face when in the presence of men, but removed it when in the presence of God, thereby absorbing more and more of God's likeness—being changed "from glory to glory."

There is no one experience in which we become like Jesus. It is a progressive work. It continues as we behold the countenance of the Lord. Its change is so gradual as to go almost unnoticed by the worshiper; he often must depend on the testimony of others to know how vastly he has changed. But he will change, for that is the ministry of the Spirit of the Lord.

For many years I stumbled over Hebrews 12:14— ". . . holiness, without which no man shall see the Lord"—accepting it as a condition to beholding the Lord. I felt that I had to attain the ultimate level of sanctification before I would ever be allowed to come into the presence of God. But I found too many Bible characters who saw visions of God, or heard God speak, who were far from perfection. For many of them this confrontation began a change in them that made them holy. Look at Abram the idolater, Moses the murderer, Samuel the young boy, Saul the persecutor, and many others. It was not their holiness that produced the confrontation, but that very visitation of God produced holiness in them. Is not this verse suggesting that there must be a dedication from God's side and a consecration from our side before we can come into the divine presence, but that once we do come in, we will be changed into the holiness of God? No man shall see the Lord without obtaining holiness, for that is the very essence of his nature, and He has chosen to give of himself to his worshipers.

Because of Christ's justification at Calvary, we can now come before the Father with Son-consciousness rather than sin-consciousness and be changed into the Father's image from glory to glory by the action of the Spirit of the Lord.

Although it is a process now and there is much more to be done in our lives, we have the blessed assurance of God's Word that ". . . It doth not yet appear what we shall be: but we know that, when he shall appear, we shall be like him; for we shall see him as he is. And every man that hath this hope in him purifieth himself, even as he is pure" (1 John 3:2, 3).

Notes

1. George C. Stebbins, "Take Time to Be Holy" (Hope Publishing Company).
2. Ruth Paxson, *Called Unto Holiness* (Chicago: Moody Press).
3. Adam Clark, *Commentary on the Holy Bible,* one-volume edition (Grand Rapids, Mich.: Baker Book House), p. 116.
4. Robert Jamieson, A.R. Faussett, and David Brown, *A Commentary Critical, Experimental and Practical of the Old and New Testaments,* Vol. 1 (Grand Rapids, Mich.: Wm. B. Eerdmans) p. 366
5. William Evans, *The Great Doctrines of the Bible* (Chicago: Moody Press), p. 38.
6. Ibid.
7. Judson Cornwall, *Let Us Enjoy Forgiveness* (Old Tappan, N.J.: Fleming H. Revell Company).
8. Robert Baker Girdlestone, *Synonyms of the Old Testament* (Grand Rapids, Mich.: Wm. B. Eerdmans), p. 175.
9. Ibid.
10. Kenneth S. Wuest, *Studies in the Vocabulary of the Greek New Testament* (Grand Rapids, Mich.: Wm. B. Eerdmans), p. 30.
11. James Hastings, ed., *A Dictionary of the Bible,* Vol. 2 (Edinburgh: T. & T. Clark; New York: Charles Scribner's Sons, 1900), p. 399.
12. Ibid.
13. Oswald Chambers, *My Utmost for His Highest* (New York: Dodd, Mead & Co.), p. 245.
14. John Brash, *Memorials and Correspondence,* p. 36.
15. Chambers, *My Utmost,* p. 78.
16. Evans, *Great Doctrines,* p. 164.
17. Chambers, *My Utmost,* p. 337.
18. Ibid., p. 339.
19. Charles H. Spurgeon, *Spurgeon's Expository Encyclopedia* (Grand Rapids, Mich.: Baker Book House), p. 19.
20. Chambers, *My Utmost,* p. 245.
21. Fanny J. Crosby, "Draw Me Nearer."
22. Spurgeon, pp. 29-30.
23. Paxson, *Called Unto Holiness.*
24. John Wright Follette, *Christian Character a Qualification* (Asheville, N.C.: Follette Books), pp. 5-6.
25. Judson Cornwall, *Let Us Abide* (Old Tappan, N.J.: Fleming H. Revell Company).
26. Paxson, *Called Unto Holiness.*
27. Chambers, *My Utmost,* p. 205.
28. Evans, *Great Doctrines,* p. 169.